photos by **Lon van Keulen**, text by **Lisa White**, Styling by **Carin Scheve**, graphic texts created by **Roland Buckley**

INTERIOR VIEW 14

ESSENTIAL

MOULDED

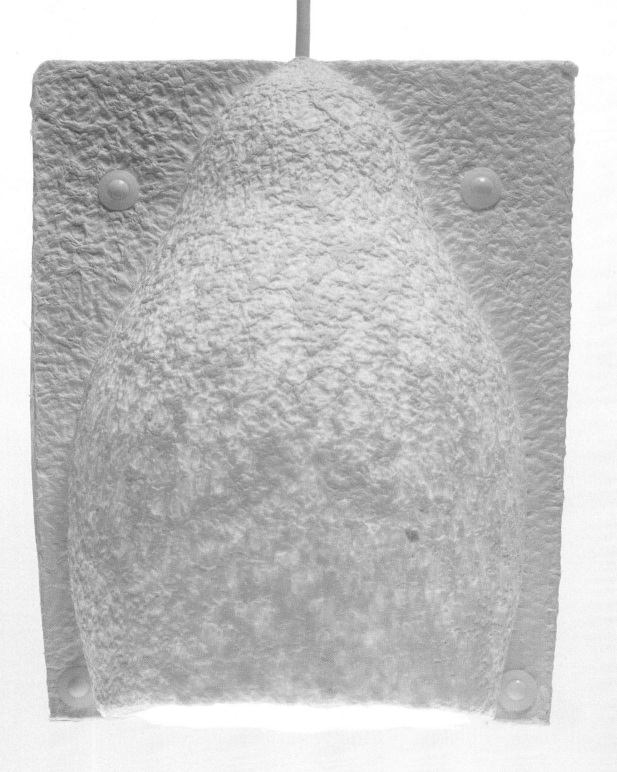

Quentin lamp by the **VK & C partnership**

brailledress and Moon text by **Shelley Fox**

7 INTERIOR VIEW 14

BLOND

ceramics by Valerie Raymond-Stempowska

INTERIOR VIEW 14

13 INTERIOR VIEW 14

INTERIOR VIEW 14

[in the raw]

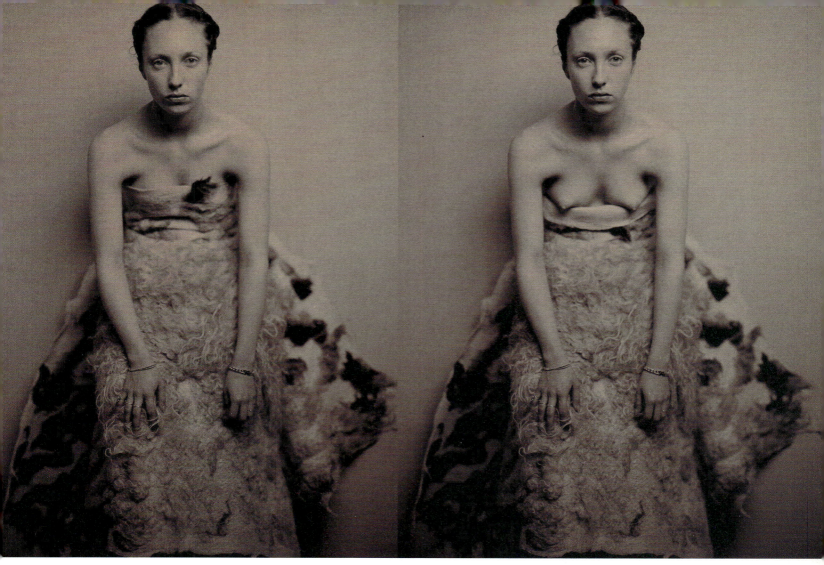

Part primitive, part animal, part magic, the felt textiles of Claudy Jongstra are unique in their rough sophistication. Some seem to come straight from the back of the beast, others are worked with a finesse that makes them a statement in raw elegance. For Jongstra uses only raw materials — raw silk, raw linen, raw camel, raw cashmere, and especially raw wool — which she then weaves and treats with original techniques that result in some of the most creative felts ever seen. Felt is her instinctive fabric, one she never tires of reinventing for clients as varied as fashion designers Donna Karan, Eskandar or Galliano, industrial designer Hella Jongerius, or the costume designers for the Jedi warriors in the next "Star Wars" film. ■ Though Jongerius has a fashion background, her interest lies deeply in the fabrication of material itself. Her call to felt came five years ago when she saw an enormous felt tent in a museum exhibition and immediately wanted to investigate its possibilities. "Basically, felt is the oldest textile in the world and thus does not have a modern image. I wanted to find out more about it to develop some contemporary versions. I want to respect its original character, its strength, so that is why I work with raw, untreated materials." Jongstra even goes so far as to raise her own sheep in the Dutch countryside and currently has a herd of 15, many of them rare European species such as the curly Gotland Pels and the long-haired Drenthe Heath, whose shorn locks she often weaves along with the straw and lanolin they accumulated on their owners. Keeping her own herd means that she can research the species and treat them particularly well to enhance the quality of their wool. Sometimes she dyes the wool, but often works with the natural variations, such as a particular brown-grey hue of alpaca that only comes about every few years. The textile edges are usually unfinished, which becomes part of the design and creates a sort of Neanderthal look when worn, as she explains "I like raw edges as well as raw materials…" ■ Jongstra's textile work is part manual, part industrial, and when machines are involved in the processing of the felt, they are often machines she has had specially made. She did not particularly want to start a production company, but in order to get the quality she needs she cannot rely on industrial weaving and must make all of her labour-intensive materials in her own atelier staffed by 10 people, including fabric designers, machine operators and a shepherd. Each fabric has its own "recipe" and Jongstra currently has a repertoire of 500 designs. More sophisticated, smoother fabrics might be a combination of alpaca, merino and silk metallic organza, while hairier, wilder ones might be a mix of merino and raw linen. Moving away from purely organic fibres, Jongstra is currently experimenting with synthetics, mixing matte wools and shiny polyesters. ■ At the Salone de Milano 99 as part of the group Dutch Individuals, Jongstra recently presented her winter fashion collection of dresses, scarves, skirts, shawls, coats for 99-00 and well as her first collection of felts for the home: blankets, cushions and upholstery, as well as a collaboration, one of four folding "Kasese chairs" created by designer Hella Jongerius. For an up-close encounter with Jongstra's felts, they can be seen at the F.I.T. or Henri Bendel's in New York, the Frozen Fountain and the Dutch Museum of Textiles in Holland, or the Egg boutique in London. Otherwise, take a close look at the Jedi and Sith on your big screens this summer…. ■ above photo *Saskia Before and After* by **Marcel Van der Vlugt** • textile photos by **Lon Van Keulen** • text by **Lisa White**. For more information, please contact Claudy Jongstra at her company "Not Tom, Dick & Harry" Openhartsteeg 1, 10017 BD Amsterdam tel 31-20 42 84 230 fax 31-20 62 09 673 e-mail NTDH@wxs.nl

composition: Alpaca, Merino, Silk metallic Organza

composition: Fiberglass, Merino

composition: Merino, Cotton muslin, Drenthe Heath wool

INTERIOR VIEW 14

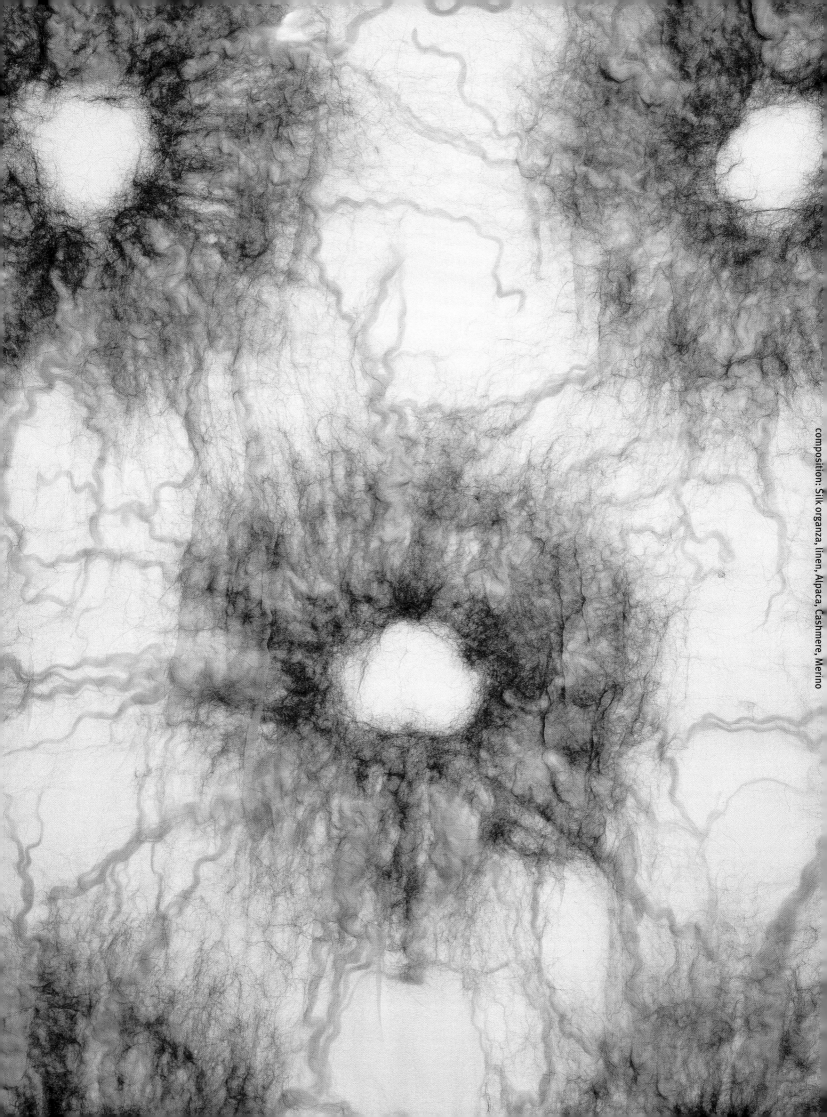

composition: Silk organza, linen, Alpaca, Cashmere, Merino

composition: Silk organza, Merino, Fiberglass

INTERIOR VIEW 14

At harvest time apples fall in the orchard, cushioned by the grass they await their destiny. Here's a little bit of this orchard feel we can bring into our homes. The fruit nest stores and cushions every piece of fruit as fresh as an English lawn. The fruit nest is made of twisted bottle brushes in various colours and shapes. After all every fruit deserves to be bedded down in its own nest.

fruit nest

On sunny days in the part or at the beach you can take this quirky ball along to play with, and besides that it's a great accessory to massage away those aches and pains, or to rub your hands and feet. The pitball is made of wood and natural bristles. 'Pitting' is a game a bit like volleyball, but when you pit the players need their quick reflexes. The one and only rule of this game is: the ball must stay air bound, no matter what it takes.

pitball

photos by **Henry Bourne**, text **Wouter Wiels** contact **Die Imaginäre Manufaktur**, Oranienstrasse 26 / 10999 Berlin • internet site: www.blindenanstalt.de

The length of the Orderly to measure makes it a great tool for professionals and the added extra helps him to brush away any rubber shavings from the desk at home or in the office.

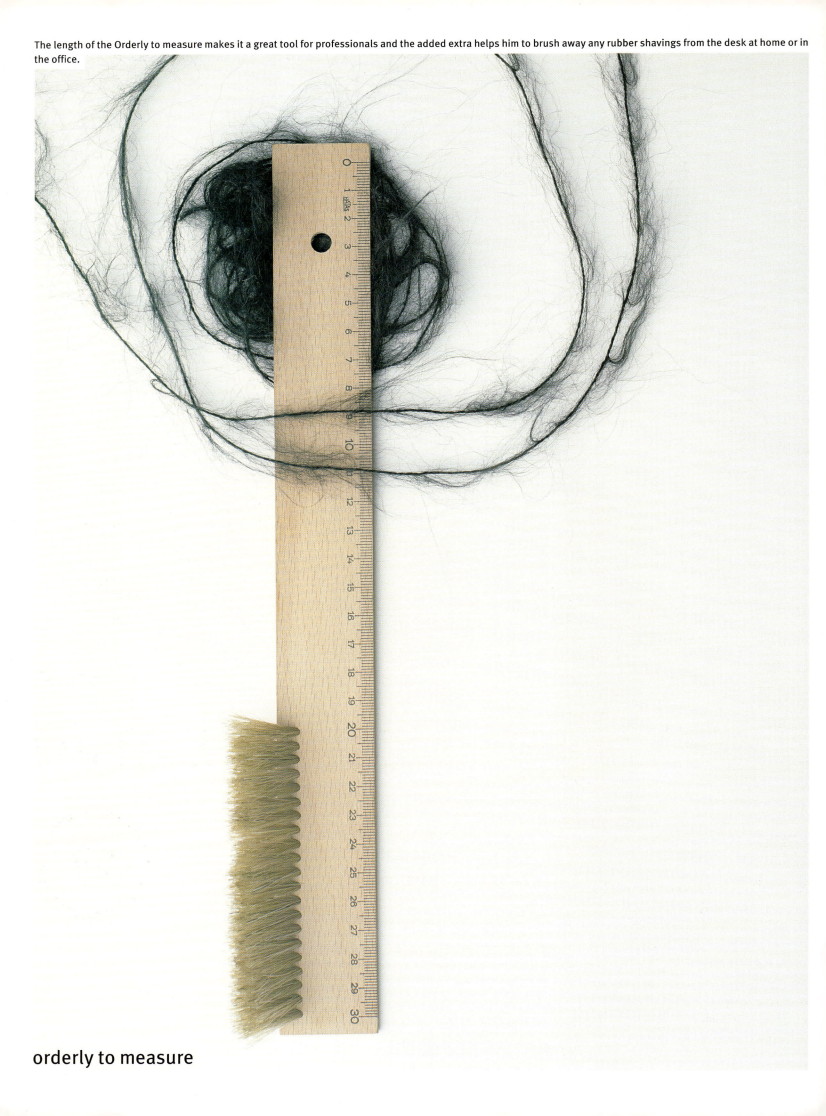

orderly to measure

Louise sprouts grass especially for freshly picked flowers so they don't droop and spring blossoms all year around. Your flowers 'll feel at home sweet home with Louise.

louise the flower tease

Vogt + Weizenegger, the studio of a Berlin based designers duo saw things right when they proposed the Berlin 'Institute of the Blind' to collaborate on the development of a new range of household products and utensils. Even while being neighbours in the same street, nothing was less obvious then that their paths would cross until it actually happened. Since 120 years, the Berlin Institute of the Blind employs blind and disabled people to manufacture classic brushes and coconut fibre doormats. Today, the fusion of the innovative design spirit and the traditional expertise of the Atelier leads to a new reality. ■ "Blind people have a special sense for shape and design and an inimitable feel for objects in front of them which they cannot see", comments Peter Bergman, Head of the Institute for the Blind. "It was a special challenge for our 50 or so blind and disabled employees to grapple with the changing needs of design and functionality. Their manual dexterity and craftmanship were a good basis for this exercise". ■ Oliver Vogt, Herman Weizenegger and 11 young designers observed the traditional methods and worked together with the blind and disabled people for several months.. ■Up to now, the 'Atelier of the Mind's Eye' has developed about 40 new products: they offer two handbrushes, one for right-handers and one specially suited for left-handers, evidence of the confidence of their approach. Another innovative development is the "egg-nest" that has flexible fibres which ensures that eggs of any size fit. The Atelier also demonstrates what you can make out of a doormat: clever use of woven-in wire means that it can be transformed into a wine rack. ■ Whether you're an innovative designer or a traditional handicraftsman, what seems to count is to stay alert for innovative impulses rather then to get rooted in normative methods.

From the second into the third dimension, Port-a-Brush, the pocketable portable brush fits flat into your wallet and its true talents are revealed whenever you need it, at once it stands in the third dimension. Here of the moment, when dust, crumbs or fluff get in the way. A customer or two has even been known to use it for their keyboard...

port-a-brush

mind's eye

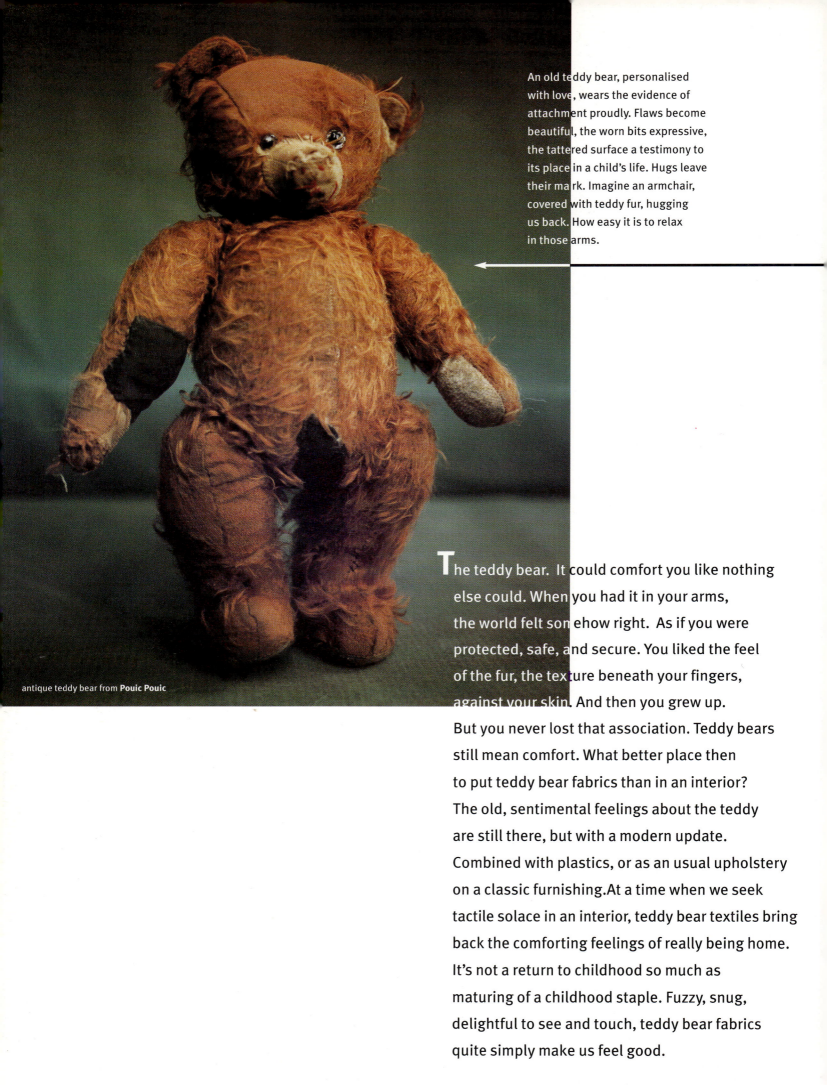

antique teddy bear from **Pouic Pouic**

An old teddy bear, personalised with love, wears the evidence of attachment proudly. Flaws become beautiful, the worn bits expressive, the tattered surface a testimony to its place in a child's life. Hugs leave their mark. Imagine an armchair, covered with teddy fur, hugging us back. How easy it is to relax in those arms.

The teddy bear. It could comfort you like nothing else could. When you had it in your arms, the world felt somehow right. As if you were protected, safe, and secure. You liked the feel of the fur, the texture beneath your fingers, against your skin. And then you grew up. But you never lost that association. Teddy bears still mean comfort. What better place then to put teddy bear fabrics than in an interior? The old, sentimental feelings about the teddy are still there, but with a modern update. Combined with plastics, or as an usual upholstery on a classic furnishing. At a time when we seek tactile solace in an interior, teddy bear textiles bring back the comforting feelings of really being home. It's not a return to childhood so much as maturing of a childhood staple. Fuzzy, snug, delightful to see and touch, teddy bear fabrics quite simply make us feel good.

Cuddle up

shirt by **Ann Demeulemeester**

photos by **Franck Heckers** @ Madé, text by **Dawn Michelle Baude**, styling by **Sara Ghazi-Tabatabai**, teddy furniture for Interior View by **Charlotte Bailly**, model **Laura Kepshire** @ Nathalies, hair by **Rodolphe Farmer** @ shack, make up by **Christina Lutz** @ Xavier Pèlaz, teddy bear textiles from **Nounours**

table from **Choupin**

Teddy bears can be modern, too. A furry tablecloth feels good against the body, brushing the skin, while the plastified table top adds an efficient update. Or encase the entire teddy-bear-upholstered table in soft, transparent plastic. Teddy is so practical.

shirt and pants by **Marcel Marongiou**

A screen, covered in teddy bear fabric, gives a warm, welcoming feel to a room at the same time that it divides up space. Straight wooden chairs, topped with furry slip covers, are both hard and soft. The structure appeals to our sense of modernity while the teddy bear fabric takes the edge off.

dress by **Lee Young Hee**, chair from **Choupin**

the paper touch

You've done it yourself — stroked an object covered in fur. But did you ever caress an envelop? A cardboard tube? Most of us view paper as a passage to something else. The blank sheet provides infinite possibilities, but it's made to be thrown away. And we do throw it away, by the tons. Newspapers, magazines, sugar cube wrappers — it all goes by the wayside. It's so banal, so ordinary. We think about recycling when we can. But with the exception of books and "important papers" — archived for their content more often

than for their form—we rapidly dismiss the majority of our paper products from both sight and mind. Pierre Pozzi set out to rectify this situation by ennobling a material so much a part of our lives that we sometimes don't even notice it's there. Pozzi wants you to feel your paper the way you feel fur, so he's designed a range of paper products which elicit touch as spontaneously as they elicit your attention. ■ His paper fur, for example, flutters, moves, palpitates. It seems almost alive, as if it were some recently introduced

species, discreetly posing on the table. Or maybe it's a new form of shrubbery—unassuming and natural. It fits so easily into the domestic landscape that it seems as if it's been there all along... ■ And it has. Using paper for domestic objects and in the living space is a tradition in Japan and in other countries. Pozzi asked himself why the same thing couldn't occur on the Western side of the world. His paper containers—understated squares, bowls and containers—are beautiful to look at without drawing undue attention

to themselves. They stack, they sit, they hold fruit or nuts or flatware or notes. As a practical material, paper is much more durable than we've been conditioned to believe. Although Pozzi works with colour, many of his designs stick to the neutrals—white, grey, cream, brown. Variations on the *papier maché* process—incorporating cotton fibres, for example—provide a continuity in the technique. "I'm working against the idea that paper is ephemeral," he says. "Paper products can last a long, long time."

When Pierre Charpin and his students at the French Regional School of Fine Arts at Rheims set out to design a car, they didn't want to create a sculptural object. No sexy surrogates, no pretentious calling cards for wealth, and above all, no flashy look-at-me power symbols. A car which would draw attention to itself was the last thing they wanted to make. Beginning from the assumption of "weak design"—which shifts the point-of-view from object to context—Charpin and his team sought for ways to blend the car into its urban environment. ■ The city, as we know, is a matrix of stimulation—sights and sounds fill the nervous system to overload, to the point that we walk around with our senses partially shut down. Both visually and acoustically, cars are an essential part of this rousing urban complex, ferrying us from one place to the next as we struggle to keep pace with our hectic schedules. Usually made from a "strong design" model, they act as extensions of their drivers, a kind of shorthand to personality. The roaring red sports car, for example, all too easily suggests the amorous disposition of its owner. The social equations between a

„VROOM"

car and its driver are so well established that they function as cultural cliches. ■ Working against all that, Charpin and his students took the focus off the car in order to emphasize the interaction of the vehicle in the environment. This is where "weak" design comes in: instead of trying to reinvent or improve the formal or expressive qualities of the object—as designers often do—Charpin began from another point: the articulation of car-to-car relationships within an urban environment. ■ By putting the focus on relationships—car and car, car and street, car and pedestrians, car and architectural backdrop, etc.—Charpin and his team were able to conceive of the car in a completely different way. Furthermore, because he and his team of automotive designers came at their project as 'laymen,' their ideas were not freighted with the overload of technical expectation which burdens engineers. ■ The life-size model which is a result of their work is generic in appeal—so simple that it's apt to be overlooked, which is just what the designers sought to achieve when they focused on the car's role in a complex of social and visual relations. The loss of status for the car is a gain in status for the environment—quite literally. If cars were less apt to shout "me, me, me," greater strides might be made to power them from non-perishable resources and to find alternative, non-polluting forms of construction. "Our intention was not to design a prototype car," says Charpin, "but to materialize an idea of a car and to formulate directions for its potential design." ■

Lampshades

Meet "Promesse"—an 'A'-line porcelain bodice with a frilly skirt. Or "Angelique" whose rubber skirt is perforated with eyelets. And "Cocotte" pampered with pleats. *Haute couture* is the inspiration for these femininedressing lampshades which add new detailing to traditional forms. Even in the blindest interior we are tempted to indulge in a little decoration, with lamps that hang like fairies in skirts of light. The lampshade updates are decorative, but not overly so. Simple materials, in a range of warm neutrals, keep excess in check, while the pure forms and a few choice frills endear us to the pretty look.   photos by **Cora**, prototypes and styling by **Kirsten Schmidt** assisted by **Charlotte Bailly**

Under skirts inspire the forms that update these lampshades. In "Mystere" whimsical wing skirts, made of sheer fabric, sport wire armatures which create a layered draping. The tiny bulbs inside shine through veils of transparency. For "Fidélité" the metal armatures suggest structured Victorian skirting. The tiny bulbs inside shine like jewels.

Transparency is important in this pair of shades. In "Delphine", the porcelain form is discreetly perforated on two sides and the light shines through the holes and through the material. "Angélique" is a more dressy version, with a scalloped edge and evident perforated detailing; the compact foamrubber lets us see the light underneath. The result? These lamps funnel light at the same time the shades themselves glow.

INTERIOR VIEW 14

Pleating gives these two lampshades a conceptual japanese feel. In "Cocotte", a string of coffee filters pleats the bulb, allowing it to peak through the folds. In "Promesse", porcelain funnels are skirted with pleated fabric, providing a contrast in material and in transparency.

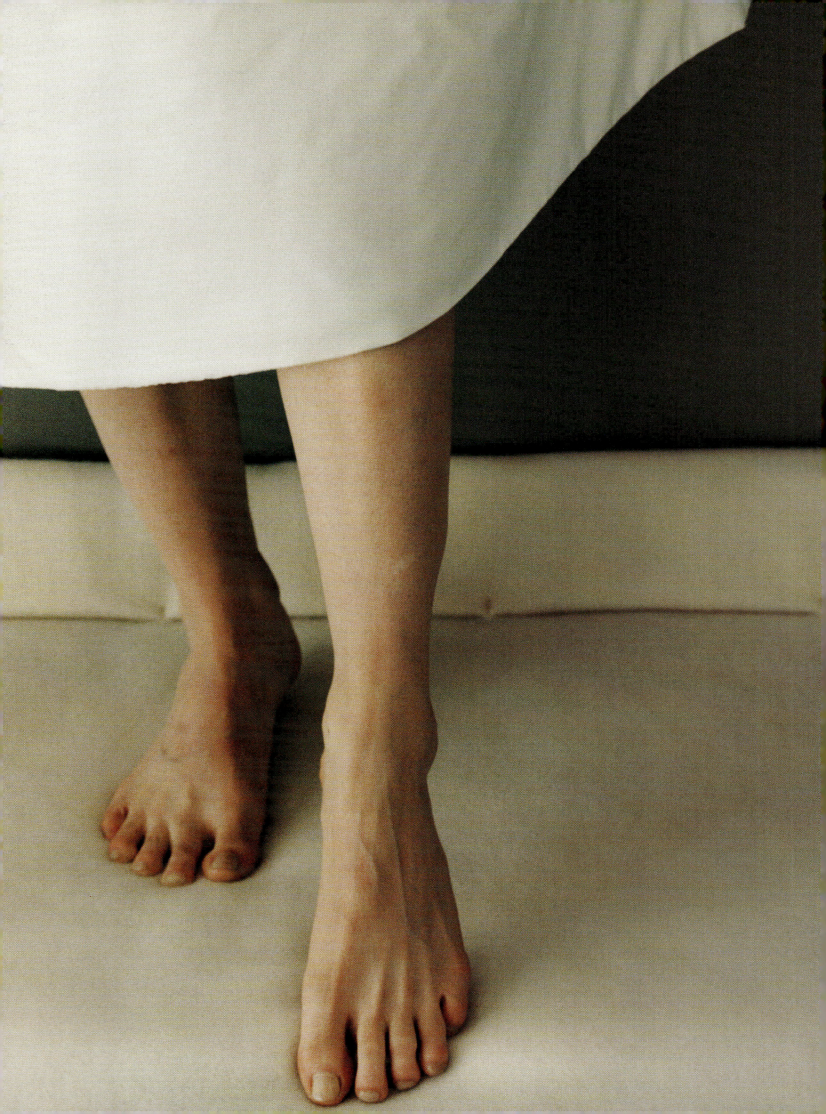

blind finishings

Technology has improved our lives in many ways, but what to do with all those cords and cables! Shove them under the table, tape them down, trip over them with a tray in your hands, try hard to keep them untangled... Here blind finishings provide a solution in the form of a blind hem. Instead of wrinkling the rug by running the cables haphazardly underneath, the 'hem' tames the confusion, rolling up and over to form a tunnel which is secured with hidden Velcro, finally concealing those cables from view. ——— at the right side, white shirt by **0918**

cable couture

That invisible touch—a concealed pocket, a hidden zip—was once reserved for only the most luxurious fashions. But these hallmarks of *haute couture* which are making inroads into sportswear are now ready to refine interior design. But in addition to the distinction of quality that meets the eye, there's something private, something hidden, something which belongs just to us. A little touch which only we know about. Or which we discover with approval. And this gives us extra pleasure. Because special attention to the details gives very special results. In soft, neutral colours—such as milk, butter, ivory and cream—blind finishings reinforce the warmth which we want from an interior.

photos by **Martyn Thompson** assisted by **Chantal Murray**, text by **Dawn Michelle Baude**, interior objects prototypes and styling by **Carin Scheve**, model **Christine Fuller** @ Viva, make up & hair by **Claudio Belizaria** @ Brigitte Hébant

private pockets

Where to put the ear plugs? the hand cream? the kleenex? We all want certain things near us when we fall asleep, if only to keep from getting up and looking around the house for our lip balm. Bedtime clutter can overwhelm a nightstand, spill out from a bedside drawer. But like hidden pockets in clothing that keep the hands free, bed pockets provide us with a tidy shelter. The hidden zip keeps your things tight. Just tuck it under the mattress and drape it down the side. The soft, cozy material blends right in.

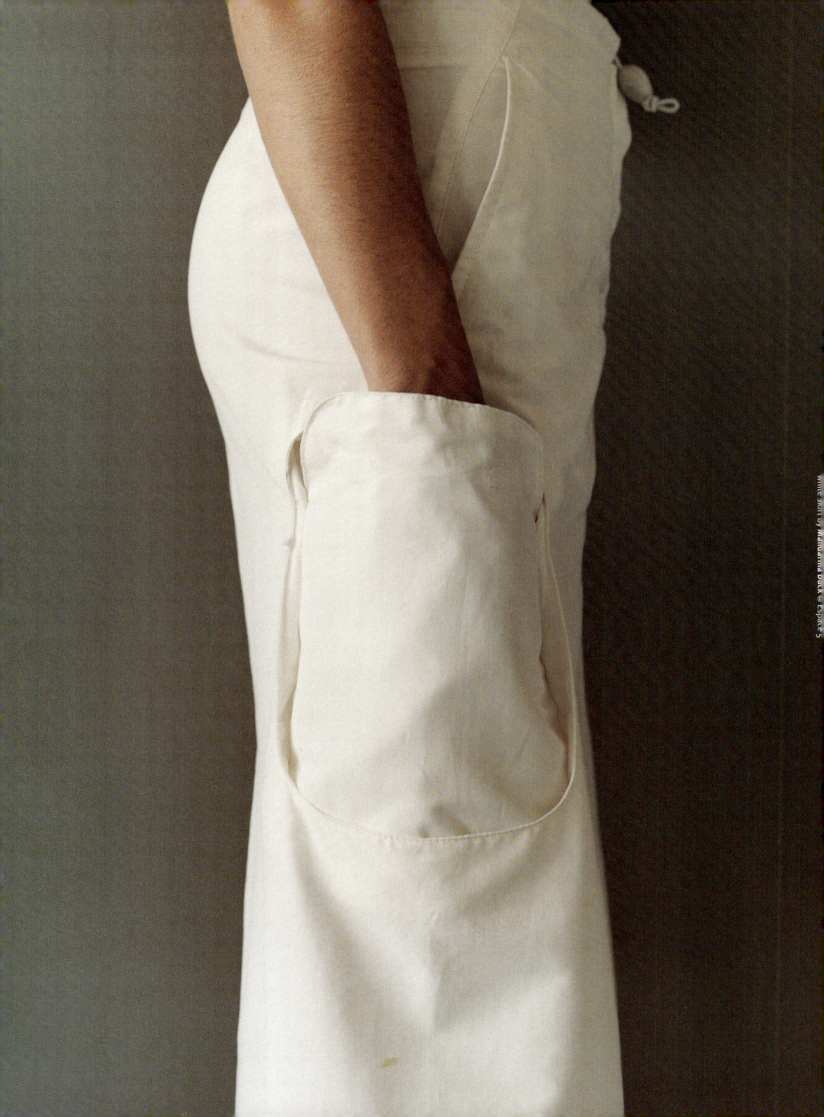

insets

Pocket insets in pants are almost invisible—you don't see them until the Velcro pulls back and the hand goes in. The same thing holds true for an interior. Fabric-covered cupboards with inset pockets steamline bedding, linens and towels. And anything else that you need to put away, out of view. By creating a kind of port-hole effect, the only thing that you see is the form until you 'open' it up. The perforated stitching on the outside keeps things simple, understated and clean.

out of sight Just as a blind finishing is said to be 'invisible', so are transparent pockets concealed until you put something inside. And what better place for a see-through pocket than in the edge of a tablecloth? The transparent material enhances and protects the table, while the pocket in the side holds the clutter until it's needed. Serving spoons, for example, or extra napkins. Practically stowed away until they're removed. And then the pocket disappears.

51
INTERIOR VIEW 14

plastic wood

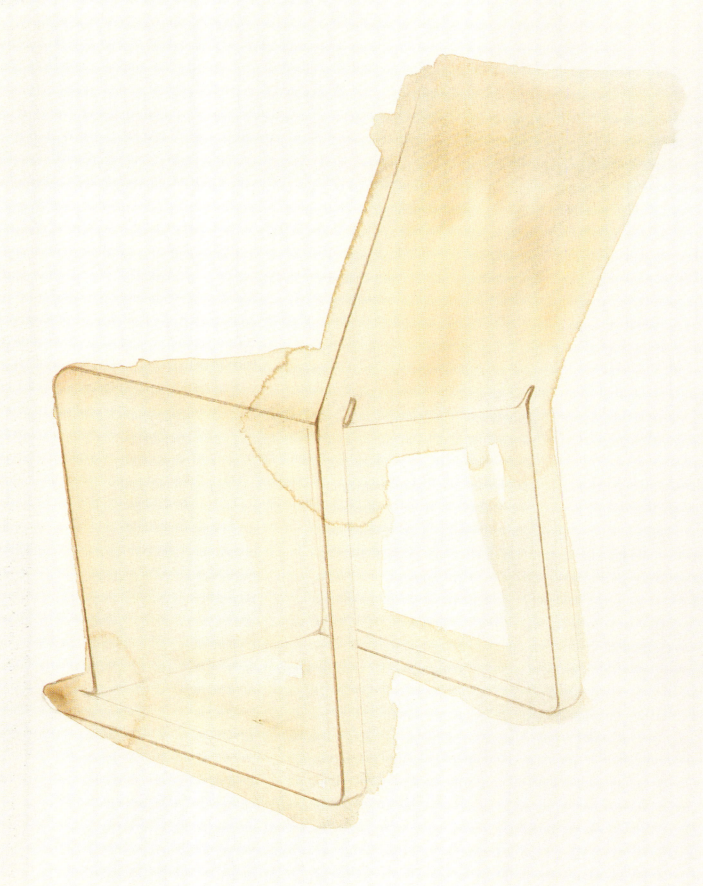

Watercolours by Karine Jollet

Illustrations by **Karine Jollet**

W O O D

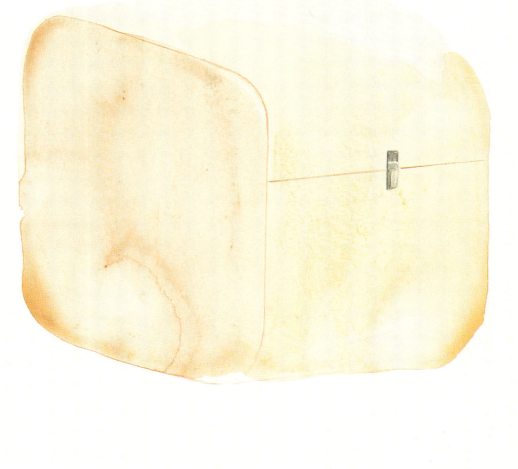

Wood in its natural state is crying out for new treatment: don't cut it, don't angle it, don't nail it - just mould it. ■ To create tomorrow's design, wood is treated like plastic, following its natural movement and grain, it is bent and formed to give rounded and curvaceous forms. ■ Taking the lead from this perfectly formed case, "fatty containers" designed by Harri Koskinen for Schmidingermodul in Austria and sublime folded chair by Iform in Sweden, Karine Jollet has imagined a portfolio of designs for this underused technique. ■ These new shapes call for a refreshing colour range of blond woods.

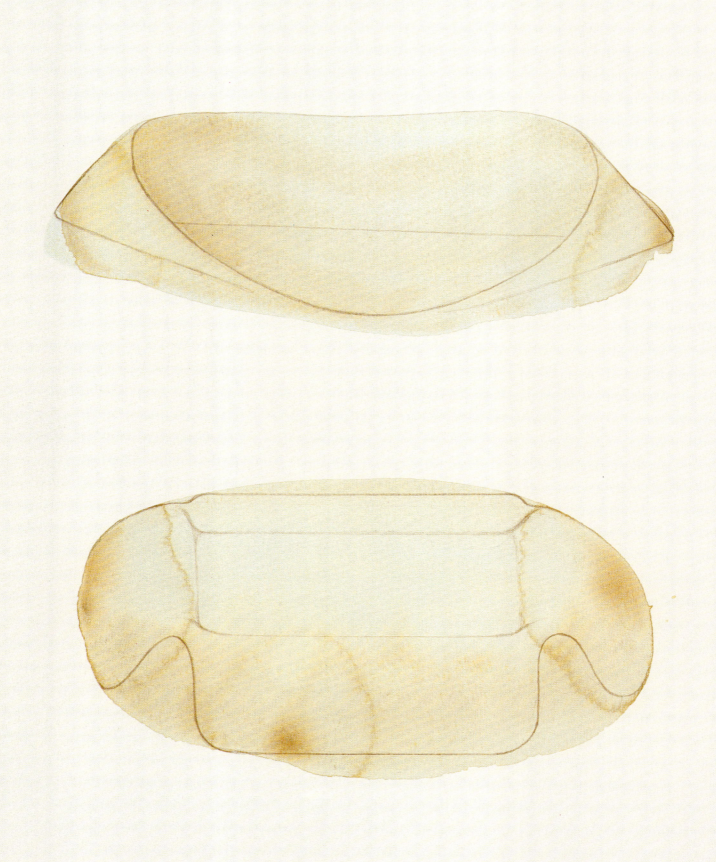

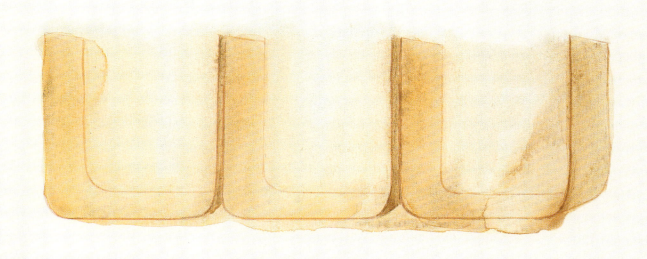

ledge forms

reclining planes

59

INTERIOR VIEW 14

Rigid, transparent Perspex casing defines the wooden form in Andreas Aas' table at the same time that it rounds off the edges. The lines of the inner object are thrown into high relief, while the form itself is blunted. We're somehow brought closer to the table as a table without dealing with it directly. The form of the transparent casing deflects our attention from the object at the same time that it reinforces its "tableness".

photos by **Lon van Keulen**, text by **Dawn Michelle Baude**

indirect vision

Now you see it, now you don't. ■ Transparency is one of the most intriguing visual strategies in an interior, because it creates a kind of unifying screen. The object is still present, but at once decisively removed. It's indirect, inaccessible. Which only increases our desire to really see and touch it. If only we could. ■ Because transparent casings filter our vision as much as they filter our touch, the object becomes new, almost reinvented. The fact that it's protected only makes it more precious. Our attention is piqued through the mystery. ■ As a levelling force, transparency can be used to blend disparate objects into a cohesive whole. The individuality of the various elements recedes as the surface comes forward. And yet, the object is more present than ever. There and not there. ■ Transparency always contains the double proposition of reification and anonymity. Simple and complex. Flatness and depth. Transparency lets us through the screen only to bring us back to itself.

Transparent tape gives Marcel Pott's furniture a soft, see-through quality. The six chairs are combined in a single wardrobe. Two other chairs are added to a frame to make an office table. The tape creates a transparent cocoon, transforming familiar stand-bys into a diaphanous nest.

light transformer

Some designers like to 'put' light somewhere. Not Arik Levy. He wants consumers to interact with light — make it move, change, shift. Maybe that's because for Levy light is almost alive; certainly he cannot resist jumping up from the table, adjusting a lamp or moving a light source to demonstrate a principle. No wonder he wears a track suit to work. Part athlete, part scientist and part metaphysician fused into one, Levy the designer can adhere dancers to the wall on the one hand and conceive phosphorescent 'windows' with the other. ■ Born in Tel Aviv in 1963, Levy first won recognition as an accomplished surfer. In his twenties, he began to design surf wear before love beckoned him to Switzerland where he attended design school in 1989. The fact that he was an older student gave him the extra thoughtfulness which attracted the attention of Seiko Epson Inc. After winning a design competition, he moved temporarily to Japan.■ The next stop was Paris, France, where one day he picked up some honeycomb cardboard lying around the studio and rolled it into the cylindrical prototype for the prize-winning lamp series, "Need," housed in the MOMA permanent collection. Other attention-getting lamp designs, such as the versatile "Seed" lamp which can hang or sit (singly or in pairs), followed, and in 1997, Levy and fellow designer Pippo Lioni founded "L" Design. The same year, Levy showed his lamps in the "Light Light" exhibition, held in Paris at the Passage de Retz. He has also developed an interactive watch prototype for Seiko that gives time new dimensions, making it tactile through raised numbers and visible through a unique process that translates excess energy from the wearer into photographic material. ■ As time passes, his lights are becoming increasingly immaterial. In addition to the innovative "White Hole" sheet lights (made from phosphorescent panels), Levy is also known for his "Alchemy" lamps — Pyrex beakers in which a low-wattage bulb is reflected through hundreds of tiny glass spheres. In his prize-winning "Cloud" series, made of stainless steel woven-fibre pockets, the light seems to float inside its envelope, while the "Rewindable Light" is simply a video of a light bulb (which can be dimmed or brightened with the TV's remote control) that runs for an hour, to be extinguished or rewound by the VCR. Below Levy talks to Interior View about the nature of light and design...

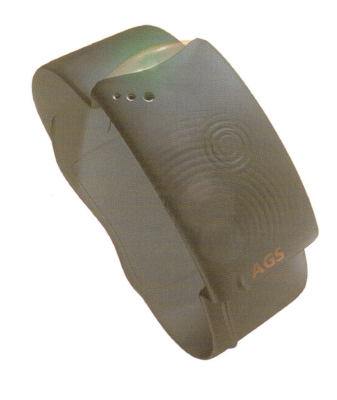

What is your earliest memory of light? ▶ I grew up in Israel. We lived on the fourth floor, and I remember when I went outside getting this glare, this 'wham' from the light outside. Super-strong. White. That moment goes directly into the theatre, the experience I've had with lighting and the stage. **What other impressions led you to become fascinated by light?** ▶ Well, I'm basically a beach bum—I'm a surfer. The morning light when you go surfing is so perfect—very early in the day, just at that moment when it's very atmospheric—the sun coming up over the water. And the desert, too. These are very contrasted... Light and water—and light and air. The first time I saw light travelling was the Aurora Borealis. I was in the north of Finland, and we were walking through the snow at night, and suddenly, there were these knives of light, travelling through the sky like a Star Wars film. Light really moves. It was like a swimming effect. We stood there on top of a hill for 15 minutes. It was absolutely holographic—real-time holographic. And to see this type of light moving was the strongest nature experience I've ever had in that sense. Bigger than the biggest waves. It's the first time that I could groove on the movement of light without imagining all kinds of physical formula. **Is light for you a substance?** ▶ Absolutely. **We usually think of light as 'immaterial.'** ▶ For me, it comes from somewhere else. It's the determination of space, of architecture—of space or no space. Without light, space doesn't exist. Without it, we can't see there's a wall or a door. There are no shadows, no forms. Every object has its natural centre of gravity. When you put a light on, you change the space. You can change the room if you put the light on one side or the other. You can change the gravity. So it is a substance although it's immaterial. It weighs nothing. **So our perceptions change as the light changes.** ▶ Absolutely. For example, these "White Holes"—they're the third type of light form that exists. We're used to the shape and space of the light bulb, and the florescent, which is linear. And now, these are new 'surface' lights—all the former notions that we have of 'shades' are completely gone. There is no lampshade. **How does it work?** ▶ Arik starts as a liquid, a phosphorescent mixture which is silk-screened on a conductive surface. Which is why we can combine them in panels but the actual size of each panel is limited. The screens can only get so big, or you have problems with it starting to dry out at one end. As the phosphorescence is a little greenish, I put red on it so that the lights look pink when not lit, and absolutely white when lit. We separate the colour spectrum, and it becomes this scientific whitish halo. So it's from liquid to surface to this new substance. **You're giving a new dimension to light, opening up a new perspective...** ▶ In the case of the "White Holes," it's bringing something which is totally scientific into a domestic space. It's a white hole like a black hole. You sit in front of it and you go into it. You create space. You put it on the wall, and it's absolutely flat, but when it's lit, it's Alice in Wonderland. There's a space. It's magical. But when you look at it and it's not lit, there's no space. **So you're moving to lamps which are less material. Instead of having a bulb, you have a hole.** ▶ I don't know how to make 'beautiful' objects in that sense. I can't go sculpt the thing and say "look at this beautiful lamp." What is beautiful in what I do is the material, the relationship between the light, the light source and the material itself—the microcosms, the microspace, the dynamic of the elements. Lights change according to the angle that you see them. light has a form, like a chair. It doesn't have a life of itself beyond what its form means to me. **But a lamp like "Alchemy," in which you**

angle the light source however you want in the beads.... ► It's your lamp. You move the bulb in the beads as you like. Someone comes into your house and moves it a little differently and you say, "why did you do that? It's my lamp." It becomes a discussion which doesn't exist in other objects. This is what I'm interested in. With titles like "White Hole," and "Need," and "Alchemy," are you alluding to metaphysics? ► Yes—it's back to what I said about substance. I'm getting to the thing, not because of the need to make a light, of the need to make an object, but because of the need to know the material. I invent materials on the biochemical level, even though I'm neither a physicist nor a biochemist—I deal with the molecular level. That is interesting. But when I go back, say, to the idea of "Need," well, everybody needs a light. There's one that's straight and the one that's curvy. And some people have little needs and some people have big needs. Do they need your light? ► They don't know. That's the thing about these lights—they are difficult for people to take home, because it's easier to go to a big department store and buy a ceramic thing with a shade because they're used to seeing it—they saw it in their childhood, and at their friends'. The "Alchemy" lamp, for example—some people who've spent time in a hospital have a hard time with it, because of the beaker. But I'm not interested in that. It's an element which I use so it disappears, because everybody knows it and there's no discussion. It is what it is, and it was done for something very simple. And what comes out is only the light. The wire is there—I don't try to hide anything. There's no apology. There's no light without electricity, apart from radiation or phosphorescence or something like that. The important thing is to get to the quality of the light and not to the object itself. Then you can have more or less fun,

sing it. You take the pieces and you put together your own lamp. And how did you decide on the honeycomb cardboard material for "Need"? ► This material has existed for 30 years—it's in every door, inside the door. The company that makes this material produces a thing that disappears. The "Need" lamp makes their material visible, and this makes them happy. It's absolutely ridiculous, because of the turnover they do, but everybody's happy. Is one of the things you do shedding new light on familiar materials? Taking base materials and making them noble? ► : It's not necessarily when the material is finished—it's just the step before. I've taken it and given it another function, another life, and it becomes a new material in itself. One brings another and it brings about a transformation. And I go to the company and I say could you do it this way? And they say no and then they say yes, and then we find things together. So—it's more innovative in the process. It's less I search, I find, I put a light inside or outside and it becomes a lamp" and then I work on that. It's more intuitive—I see it, I feel it, and I start doing it. I want a "wow" effect, so you look at the object and it's a "wow." It flies. Why lamps? ► At first I thought it was easy to make a lamp, because I had never made lamps before. But it doesn't work like this at all. It's difficult. Every prototype that I do lives at home with me for at least a month, I have to look at it, how it feels and what it does, in this context and that context. After a month I ask myself what did it do? how does it look? what did my space do to the lamp? how could it change?. So for me, the objects have many different levels. And people use lamps in different ways. Like to tell time. ► Light tells a story. In Helsinki, it's very weird. Your eyes get used to the light or no light. There's a kind of bio time in which light causes confusion. Light can tell us speed—it can give us distance. The amplitude is created in experience. A chair has little amplitude, but a light source has it. It transforms. It's interactive. It transforms form. People need light and need to feel it. Are most of your things made industrially? ► Semi-industrially.. Most of the things are made industrially and then there's a manual touch. I'm a fanatic for perfection in the process. It's a sexual event. In alchemy, for example, I wanted the light to be reflected though perfect spheres so you can get the hot spot and the radiance, so that each sphere shines in a perfect way. The spheres are used sort of like filters to mix liquids, but you have to go through the bags and sort them out. So it's hand-finished. And the last touch is the consumer. Because the lamps are interactive, they're imperfect. Each one is different. Most of my lamps come as kits. What other design work do you do? ► Corporate identities, graphics, furniture, stands, interiors, and so on. I'm always looking for the "wow" effect in different ways and doses. I found a Velcro system which could hold dancers on the wall—the Velcro company said, no, it doesn't work like that, but we did it. And what about your "Rewindable" light bulb video that just came out? ► It's a kind of watch. My kid tells me, "I don't want to go to bed," and I put on the video, and I say, "when this is over, you go to bed." And what about the interactive watch? ► It tells time by voice command. It's a life watch—it works kinetically like other watches, only the overcharge of energy is stored in a micro-processor and used to power a photo cell which takes snapshots during the watch's lifetime—about 15 years. At the end of that time, you develop the negative inside the watch and you have a composite 'snapshot' portrait of your life. It's a way of touching time. It's the transformation of immaterial to material. ► And back again. interview by Lisa White and Dawn Michelle Baude, text by Dawn Michelle Baude

White Light

Light...
project into an
                                                            inte...
cube with a crisp pictograph. Light is redefining its bound...
and furniture. Material and immaterial. Background and...
an interior—supplying 'atmosphere' say—light is beco...
forms is important. Because we need to put a little order...
Or open up and embrace. Geometry is, after all, the study...

This "Galileo" lamp, designed by Arturo Silva, projects geometric shapes onto the wall, floor or ceiling of an interior. Constructed with adjustable apertures, th...
light is emitted from of the lamp and into the room in luminous shapes. The geometric forms literally shift the focus from the lamp to the material of light itsel...

s a new edge. Imagine glowing geometric forms which

. Or a sphere ra diating with luminosity. Or an illuminated
es. Between d ark and light. Light source and room. Lamp
eground. In stead of always playing a supporting role in
ng, quite literally, the focus. And the geometry of these
ur env ironment. We want to draw lines, contain, define.
relation ships between forms. And light provides the link

photo **Paul Lepreux**, styling **Carin Scheve**

Both Jasper Morrison's "GloBall" lamp for Floss (opposite) and "Gift pour Jacques" by Stokes @ Axis (this page) produce a diffuse light from clear-cut, enclosed forms. The luminosity creates auras around the lamps, while the hot points remain inaccessible and mysterious. Transparent and opaque, these lamps redefine their function as light containers.

These two lamps also function as tables. "De Light" (this page) by Elsa Frances and J.M. Policar (@ Ligne Roset selected by Via), projects radiance from an adjustable cone which can be moved around the table like a dimmer switch. Shift the cone one way, and the intensity of the light increases; slide it in the other direction, and it dims. The interactive quality implicates the owner in the form. The "Bianca" lamp (opposite), by A Quaglio and M. Simonelli (@Ligne Roset selected by VIA), provides a functional luminous surface. The purity of the form is sufficient in itself, or it can be used to actually put objects in the spotlight.

75

INTERIOR VIEW 14

Pictograms use a stylized, hard-edged image as a vehicle of communication which functions internationally, regardless of the viewer's linguistic background. As our public spaces evolve, there will be a need for new signage. These luminous pictographic lamps, by Roland Bukley, suggest symbols for our growing demands: quiet reading space, fresh water, good reception for portable phones, and Email center. (lamps: Q.BO by Artelux)

Designer Pippo Lionni conceived of his recent book, *The Facts of Life*, in order to pass on to his children the wisdom that comes through experience. The idea was to illustrate concepts through a pictographic language geared to a world which is overwhelmingly visual. Although his approach was rational—to illustrate 'eternal truths', for example—both the creation of the pictograms and their interpretation are totally subjective. Each one functions as a visual shorthand. Both amusing and provocative, Lionni's pictograms push us to reconsider our own "truths."

...."!"........."!"....."!"...."!"..."!""!""!"."?"...."?""?""?",.."?"
"?""?""!""?""?""?""!"......"!".."!"..."!"...."!""?"..."?"...:...."!"..
."!"?"...."?""?"..."!"........"?""!""?"..."?""!"......"!"......."!";....
"!"; "!","!":"!";"!","!";"!","!":"!";"?"......"!"........"?""!"....."?".
"!"..."!".."!""?""!"..."?""!"...."?"....."?""!""?""!"."!""!""!".."!"
"?"..."?"........"?"..."?".."?"......."?"..."!"......."!".."?"."?"."?"
.."!"...."!"......"!"........"!"...:........"!".............."?".."?"...."!"..
..:"!"..."?""!"...:..."!"....,"!"..."?"..."!"...."?"..."!""!"..."!""?"
.....,..."?""?""!"...."?"..."!"..."!""!""?""!"."!""!""!"."?"..."?"..
........"?"..."?".."?"......."?".."!"......."!".."?"."?"..."!"....
"!"....."!"......."!"...:.."?"..."?"......."?"..."?".."?"..........

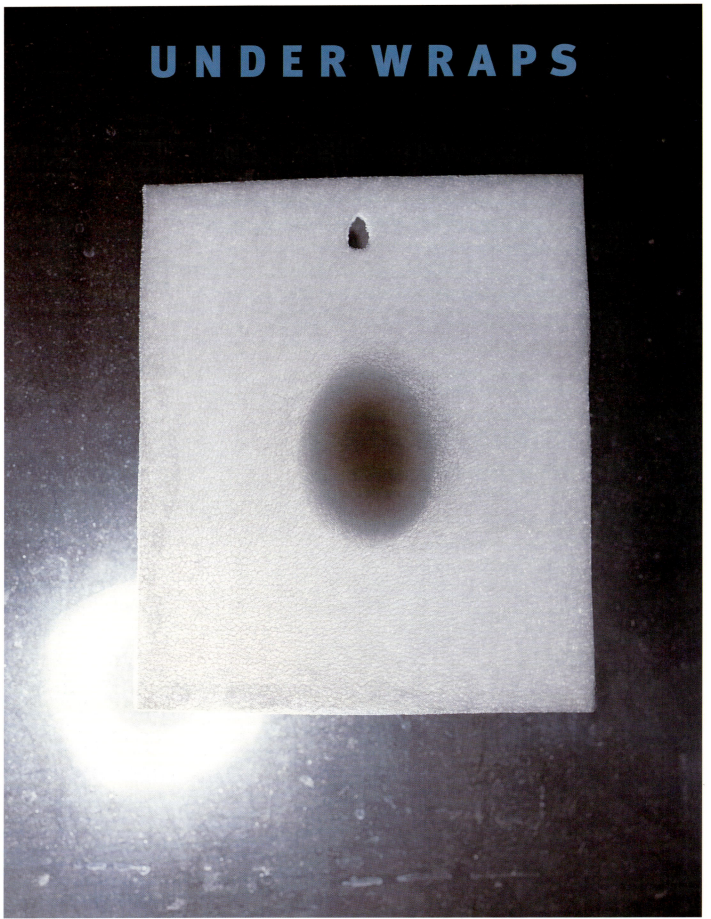

On a mass-market level, the movement towards blind design will have an important role to play in the field of packaging. Instead of products that cry out to be consumed, rivalling one another with flashy colours and logos, Interior View suggests casting a veil of translucent material over the goods to give them an aura of mystery (dare we say spirituality?), thereby elevating the everyday to the eternal. This translucent packaging can go from the technical, such as plastics and other synthetics, to the organic, such as wax, cotton, paper, ice or gelatine. Translucent treatments honestly allow us to see the goods, yet make even the most basic product beautiful. Shopping at the supermarket — or the drugstore or any store in the mall — could become a peaceful experience, with these refined generics toning down brands and honing our sensitivity to what's really inside. photos by **Stephan Abry**, styling by **Sabine Van Hest**, packaging prototypes by **Sabine Van Hest and Roland Bukley**

STORED

VEILED

a paper bag becomes waterproofed with a fine layer of wax

INTERIOR VIEW 14

ENFOLDED

SUSPENDED

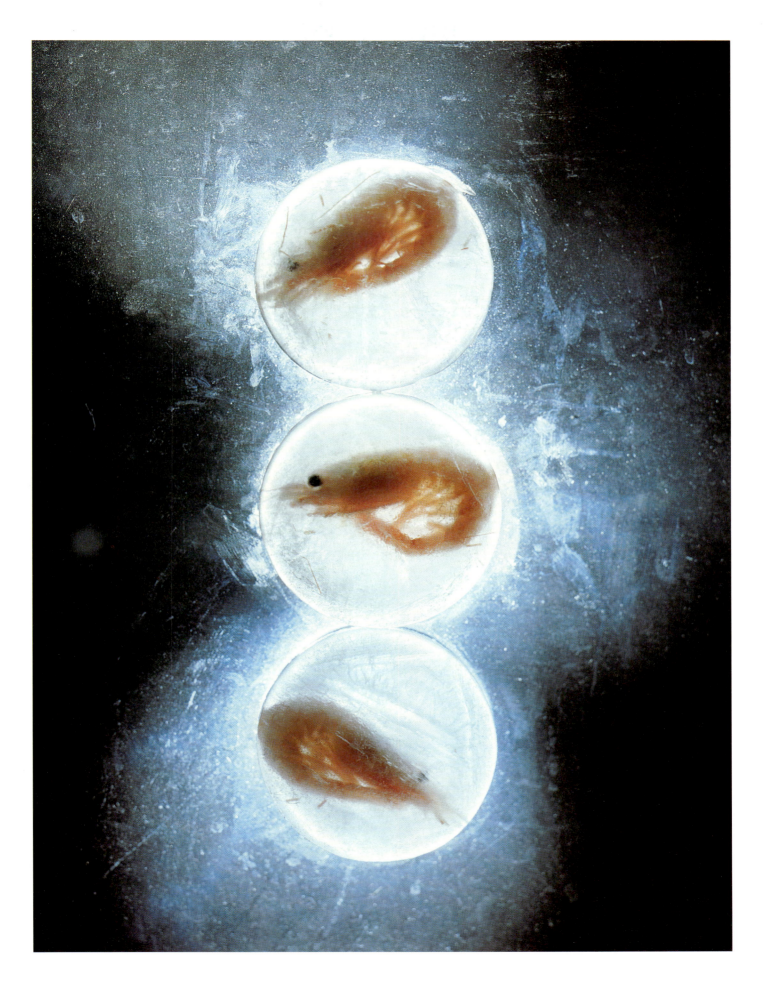

cocktail shrimps are individually packaged in ice

ENCIRCLED

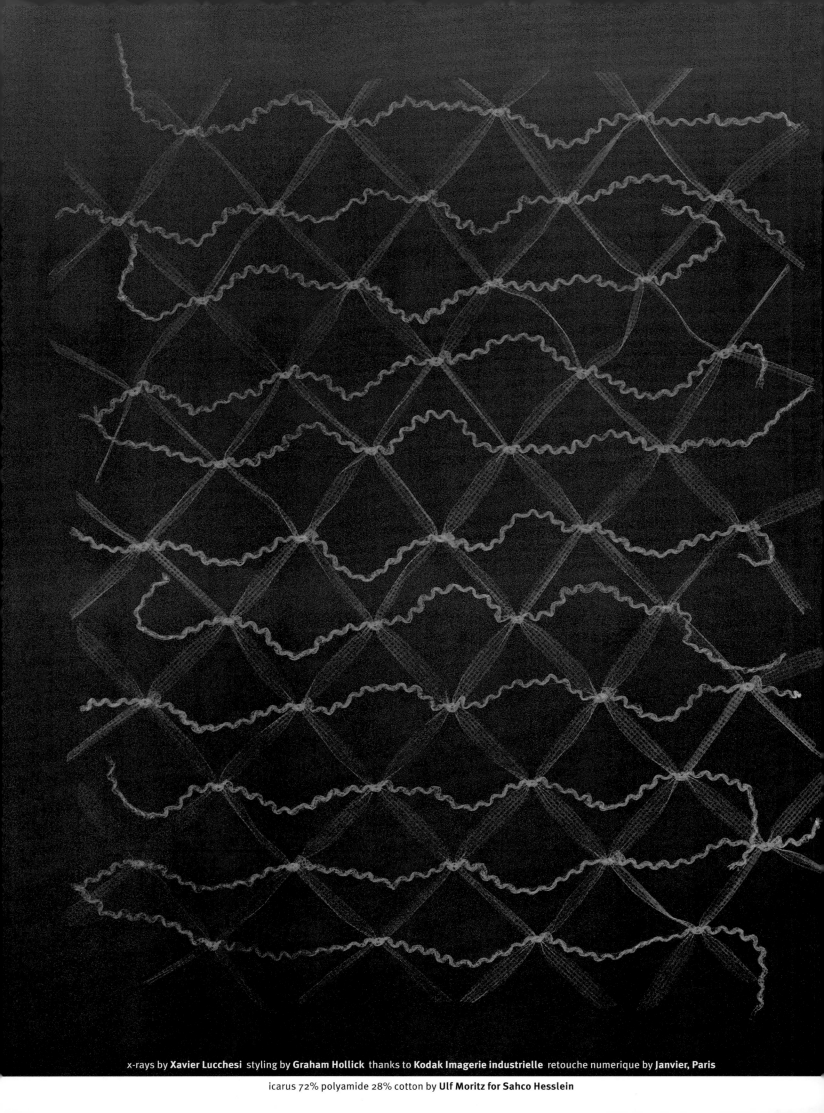

x-rays by **Xavier Lucchesi** styling by **Graham Hollick** thanks to **Kodak Imagerie industrielle** retouche numerique by **Janvier, Paris**

icarus 72% polyamide 28% cotton by **Ulf Moritz for Sahco Hesslein**

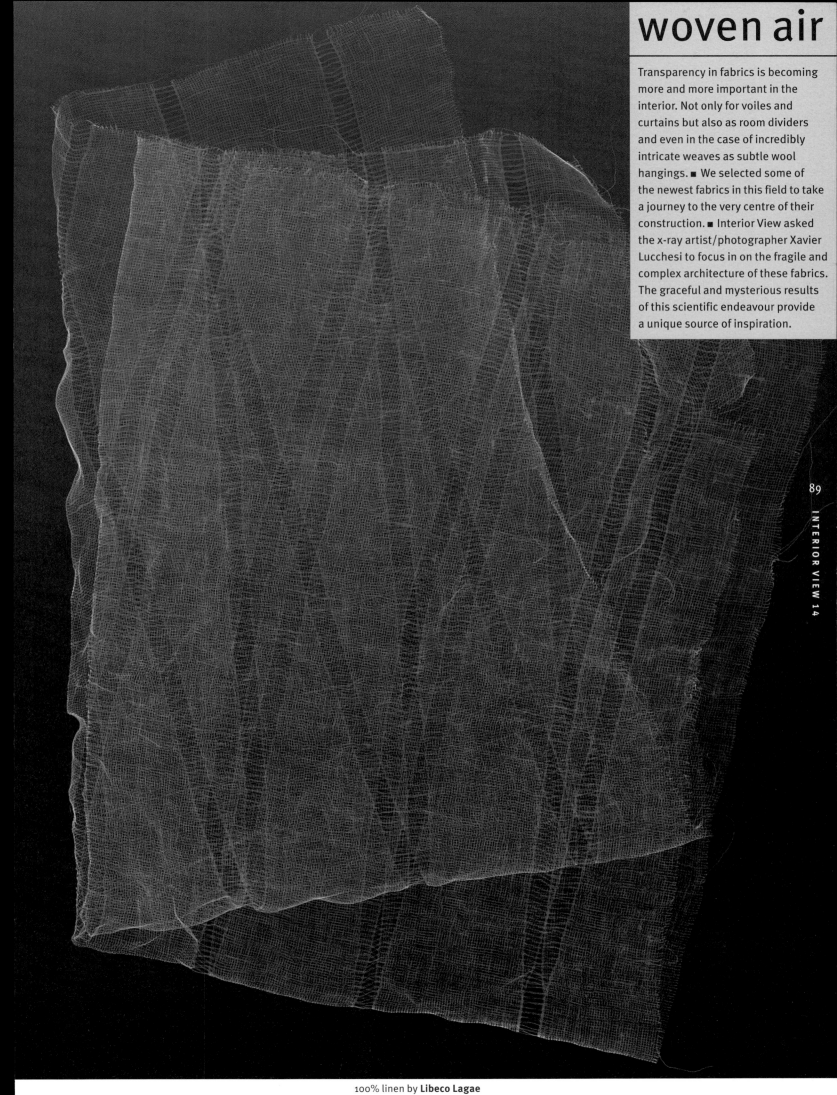

woven air

Transparency in fabrics is becoming more and more important in the interior. Not only for voiles and curtains but also as room dividers and even in the case of incredibly intricate weaves as subtle wool hangings. ■ We selected some of the newest fabrics in this field to take a journey to the very centre of their construction. ■ Interior View asked the x-ray artist/photographer Xavier Lucchesi to focus in on the fragile and complex architecture of these fabrics. The graceful and mysterious results of this scientific endeavour provide a unique source of inspiration.

100% linen by **Libeco Lagae**

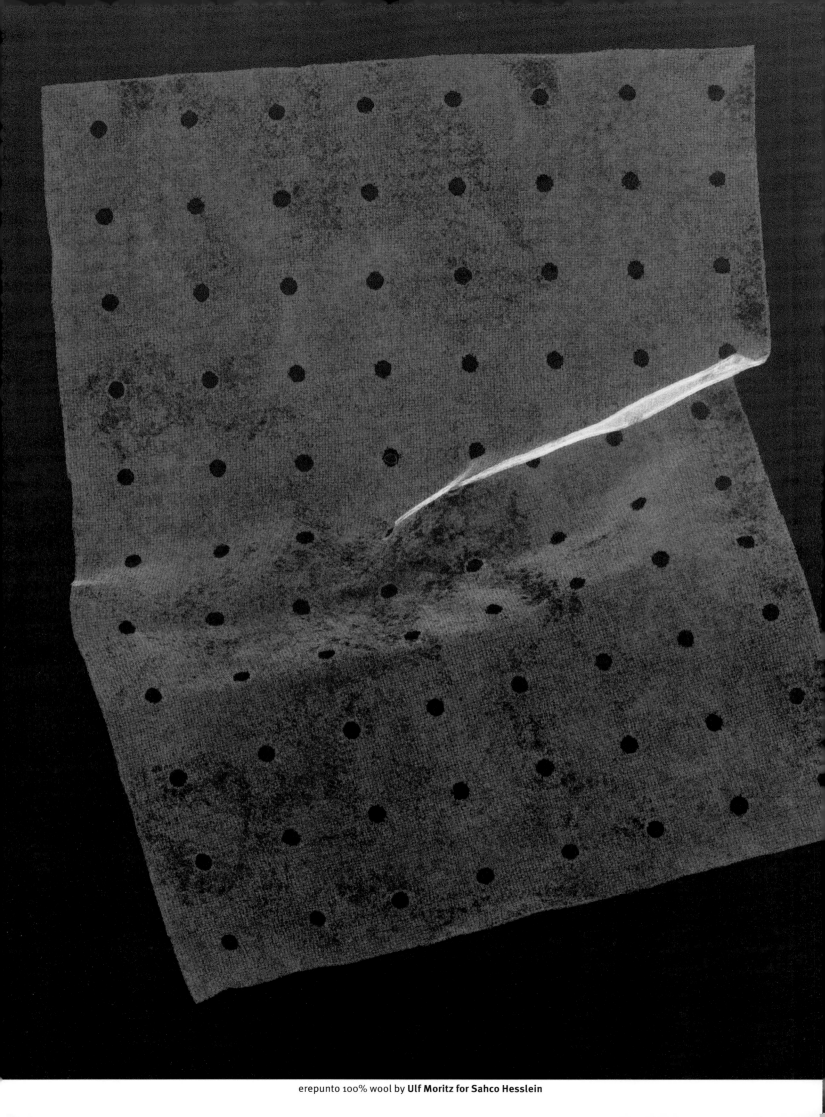
erepunto 100% wool by **Ulf Moritz for Sahco Hesslein**

safira 50% silk 42% cotton 8% polyamide by **Ulf Moritz for Sahco Hesslein**

miami 73% trevira 27% cotton by Kinnasand

mystica 65% silk 35% polyamide by **Ulf Moritz for Sahco Hesslein**

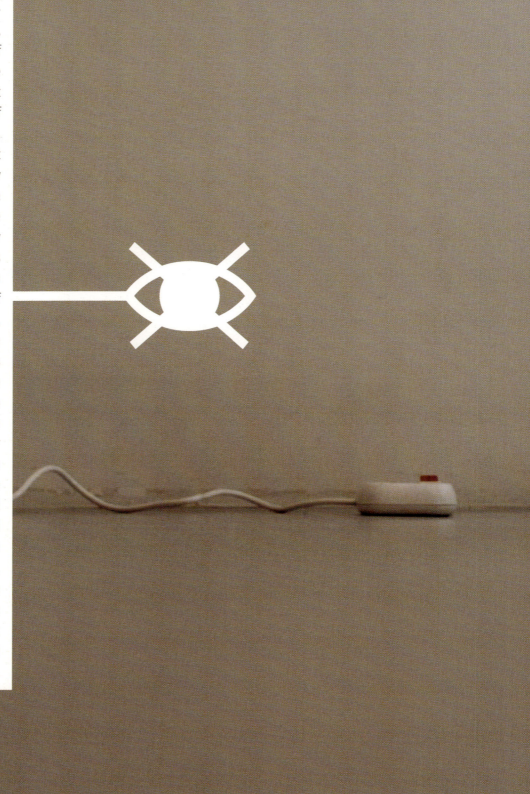

As the designers of electronics and computers have just began to open us visually to the interiors of their technical creations. Apple's i-mac and G-3 computers or the new, translucent version of Nintendo's Gameboy are helping us to appreciate what makes up the bodies of everyday technological tools. Fascinating, reassuring, what was once an absolute mystery is gradually unveiled through a layer of plasmic plastic. On the other hand, there are many technical aspects of our lives that we would prefer to screen out such as putting a layer of protection between the noise, the visions, the smells, the harsh realities of our daily lives and our sensitive souls. There are times then we would like to block out the sensorial violence that constantly demand our attention. Beginning with a visual layer of peace, we are able to retreat behind placental plastics, translucent silicas and opaque synthetics. These materials serve as blinders, making a sort of white noise that allows us to concentrate on our own inner music, and yet to focus on function and information when necessary.

prototypes and styling by **Sabine Van Hest** for Interior View photos by **Martin Müller**

screening it out

News, violence and irritating kid's programs retreat behind a soothing blur of colour, pattern and movement. But when information or entertainment is desired, the screen can be lifted away to watch the flames of your favourite program.

Time stares us in the face with unforgivable, digital truth. You're late! It's a fact. You can't escape, but you can control your stress by covering up those glaring red numbers, remaining blithely oblivious until you have get close enough to the absolute truth.

Why are all portable phones and remote controls black? — they are always getting lost anyway, so they might as well disappear behind a peaceful layer of white, with buttons and screens appearing as discreetly as Braille.

INTERIOR VIEW 14

bag from **Muji**

This translucent pod makes an embryo of whatever technical product you'd like to bring down to size. A contemporary, portable oubliette.

plate and cups by **Bodo Sperlein**

VESSEL

oil and vinegar jars by **Ron Arad** for Rosenthal

rugby cookie jar by **Ulrike Weiss**

was a touring holiday in Southern Sweden, through an area with a long tradition of glass blowing that gave Nadia Demetriou Ladas her first exposure to the colourful fifties glassware that would transform itself from being a collection to an obsession over the next four years. Friends joked that she would end up with a stall in Portobello Road Market, but at this stage it seems unlikely she can be persuaded to part with any of her precious collection at Vessel, her new glass and ceramics shop in West London. ■ Vessel is an oasis of calm and international style just minutes away from Portobello Road. The shop, which also incorporates a gallery, is described by Nadia as "a modern Mecca for those who appreciate beauty in their life, both to look at and to use" and contains a truly global selection of tableware and accessories sourced from Japan, Italy and Scandinavia, as well as from the UK. Many of the pieces are not available anywhere else in the country and the diverse range ensures that there will be something that will appeal to everyone. Everything in Vessel is carefully chosen for simplicity and versatility and as the name Vessel suggests, many of the pieces are multi-functional - they can be used to hold anything you want. ■ The last ten years has been a major change in our eating habits, both eating out and eating at home. We need tableware that reflects the different things we eat and the different ways we eat them. "Everyone is so cosmopolitan these days", Nadia comments, "We eat Thai noodles, Italian rice, sushi, couscous and we eat from bowls and on trays, sometimes sitting on the floor or on a couch." Eating in the nineties has become much less formal; the tradition of using endless different sorts of glasses and three different knives and forks is restricted to only the most formal occasions and few of us want to have a separate set of plates and glasses that is kept hidden away in glass cabinets. ■ A former music journalist, Ladas organised PR and sponsorship for her furniture designer boyfriend Angel Monzon and impressed his Japanese clients so much by the way she had styled their flat, that she was offered a dream job of becoming a buyer for their Japanese homeware company. This involved not only sourcing the best of British contemporary design for their shop, but making frequent trips to Tokyo and her first introduction to the world of Japanese culture. ■ This proved to be a major

pitcher *Papalla* by **Arcade**

nightlight *Asami* by **Arcade**

influence on Nadia, particularly the simplified Japanese way of living, ancient t ceremonies and the modular nature of Japanese various plates, bowls and boxe Nadia realised that many Eastern traditions and ideas have captured the Wes imagination and Vessel reflects this with its range of sake beakers, chop stick sushi mats and iwachu cast iron tea pots. ■ The shop is flooded with natu light and has a modern yet understated interior designed by Angel. It featur simple glass and elm cabinets, muted colours and slate floors and acts as t perfect backdrop for Nadia's carefully chosen collection. ■ Highlights inclu elegant ceramics by Ikebana and glowing heart shaped vases by Saliva bulbous spice shakers by Arabia, beautifully simple bone china from Bo Sperlein, funky flower plates by Driade, Orrefors' classic relaunched 1953 gla Fuga bowl and the stunning white Yao vase by recent graduate Kazuhiko Tomi for Arcade. As well as glass and ceramics, Vessel stocks delicately curv wooden trays in birch and walnut veneer that can double as placemats, simp stainless steel cutlery from Hackman Tools and Rosenthal and other intrigui accessories for living such as Danish cheese slices, candle holders and schnapps set with conical shaped glasses that forbid any polite sipping. ■ T first exhibition in the spacious downstairs gallery space will be 'The Relatio Project' from Finnish glassware company Iittala. This is the first opportunity see Marc Newson's curvy glasses, Constantine Griec's affordable beakers, Kari Seph-Andersson's stacking bowls, Annaleena Hakatie's pitchers and Ha Koskinen's exquisite hourglass candle holder. The space will be used showcase more experimental pieces by young designers and also serves an area for customers to relax, with its comfortable seating and the offer complimentary jasmine tea. ■ Nadia spends a lot of time talking to h customers and has succeeded in creating an informal atmosphere that h attracted a wonderfully diverse range of people - everyone can come away wi something, whether it's a £600 vase or a simple sushi mat for £2. Nadia is passionate about the people who use her objects as she is about the iter themselves. She hopes that each piece in Vessel will bring pleasure to anyo who uses it and comments, "It's all about injecting some art into everyday life

Yao vase by **Kazuhiko Tomita**

culinary visions

"Everyone to the table!" And what wonderful times we have—gabbing with friends and family, savouring fantastic food and a robust glass of wine. Meal times are the one moment of the day when we settle down and genuinely relax, forgetting the post-its and to-do lists, the traffic jams and the all-pervasive stress of life at the turn of the millennium. Inhaling the heady scent of a spicy vegetable sauté we feel, well, human again. In fact, one way of increasing the quality of life is by increasing mealtime pleasure—which may seem difficult to do when the demands of work and home put a premium on our time. But here's where technology comes to the rescue. Or at least gives us a helping hand. Not by de-humanizing the domestic space, but by re-humanizing it with unobstrusive appliances as easy to use as they are to look at. Visionary products which affirm our most cherished values and help us create new rituals that correspond to contemporary culture.

Preparing the Future Meal The new generation of culinary wizardry takes the restaurant—or the chateau!—as its model. Either way, there's an army of folks employed to do one thing: make your meal memorable. In the home, this translates into the following—minimizing time spent in the kitchen and maximizing time spent together at the table. By developing the right kinds of high-tech products, we can enhance, rather than compromise, traditional attitudes toward food. ■ Take the linen tablecloth 1 —a standard of many a mealtime revery— but this time, make it interactive. Plug it in—quite literally. The inductive, cable-free power integrated into the fabric can keep a pasta dish warm, but without putting the guests at risk. Special ceramic dishes concentrate the heat where you want it. When it's no longer necessary to keep food toasty in the oven or to find a moment to reheat it, you'll be able to spend more time with your guests and less time carrying trays.

■ And since being together is what really counts, look for new cordless group-cooking tools. Using halogen heating elements, the next generation of attractive, simple skillets will sit directly on the table 2. The soft patterns of light add to the atmosphere of the evening, while the sights and smells of fondue, raclette or barbecued chicken make everyone's mouth water.

2

3

4

Sensual Technology Although the delights of the senses might seem to be diametrically opposed to the efficiency of microchips, wetwear and hardware are becoming more compatible. New wine conditioners, for example, 'know' that in order for you to enjoy your wine, it has to be kept at the right temperature. The conditioner reads the bar code on the bottle, and sets itself accordingly. 3 The proper temperature is maintained, in turn, by the glass, so that the fullness of the flavour remains constant. ■ Because we want our technology to do its job without drawing attention to itself, the conditioner is designed as a discreet glass sheathe. Similarly, the latest design in audio systems—a ceramic chip player and microphone is understated, intentionally simple, almost pure. The player is the size of grapefruit —it sits, white and shiny, like a piece of crockery on the table. When you lift the lid, you can drop in four music chips to program the evening's melodies. The speakers hang on the wall like plates. 4
all prototypes developped by Philips

5 6 7

Time In Bed A week-end breakfast in bed personalizes the luxury of a good meal. There's nothing like enjoying a good cup of coffee and taking the time to catch up on the news. Wooden breakfast trays with magnetic metal contacts not only keep hot things hot and cold things cold, they also prevent slippage, so if you tilt the tray to plump a pillow, your orange juice won't fall over. A small, removable wooden screen attaches to the tray. With a touch of a finger, you can read your E-mail or step out on the internet. The cushioned tray base fits snugly across the lap, reminding you that you're at home in bed, not at the office. 8

■ Expect to see more windows of the future in the kitchen too, with recipe screens illustrating new cuisine ideas or recalling your favourite dishes. Drop in the 'fish' chip for example, and up pops the step-by-step instructions for a basted filet or marinated Coquille St. Jacques. 5

Keeping An Eye On Food The window idea extends, as well, the staples of the kitchen. 5 Transparent glass toasters will allow us to see the bread toasting, while transparent glass kettles will let us watch the water boil. 7 The kettle comes with a special filter to purify the water as it's poured. Since keeping food fresh is a necessity, glass micro-climate containers will regulate both temperature and humidity, so the goat cheese you have for lunch is as perfect as it was when it came from the market. 6 ■ In order to have more control over what you eat outside the home, health monitors, fashioned like chopsticks, will test foodstuffs for the presence of specific allergens when eating in restaurants or while travelling.

The cotton news is softer, fleecier, cozier, and, well... woollier. Using slubbed fibres—in which the thickness of the strand varies—cotton takes on a new texture. By replacing the stiff, dry, crisp features of cotton with the softer, more comforting characteristics of wool, we can enhance the part of cotton that we adore—its light weight, durability, and porousness—with the protective, luxurious aspects of the wools that we crave. ■ Think of a couch and chairs, upholstered in a furry cotton, which invite us to sit down. Or quilted cottons, plush and softly padded, giving that extra ease to pillows, cushions and throws. The added volume in flannel sheets and terry towelling will make us feel even more pampered. Double-weaves, jerseys, and multi-ply—for curtains, blankets and tablecloths—send a comforting signal. At a time when we need more than ever to relax in our homes, woolly cottons can supply a visual and tactile signal that we're protected. By becoming thicker and softer, cotton keeps us snug and warm.

What better way to treat cotton than as wool?

photos by **Lon van Keulen,** text by **Dawn Michelle Baude,** sheep shears from **BHV**, Paris

Post-it
When you have all the time in the world and a playful mind to match it you'll have a ball sticking new Post-it's on the window and removing others that suddenly loose their attraction. Subtle and funny. Never a dull moment for lighthearted sunchasers and shadowplayers at home or at work.

photos by **Fred de Gasquet**, text by **Marie Jeanne Rooij**, prototypes and styling by **Veerle Hommelen**, fabric by **Kinnasand**, glue stick by Papercraft de Vernantes

blinds

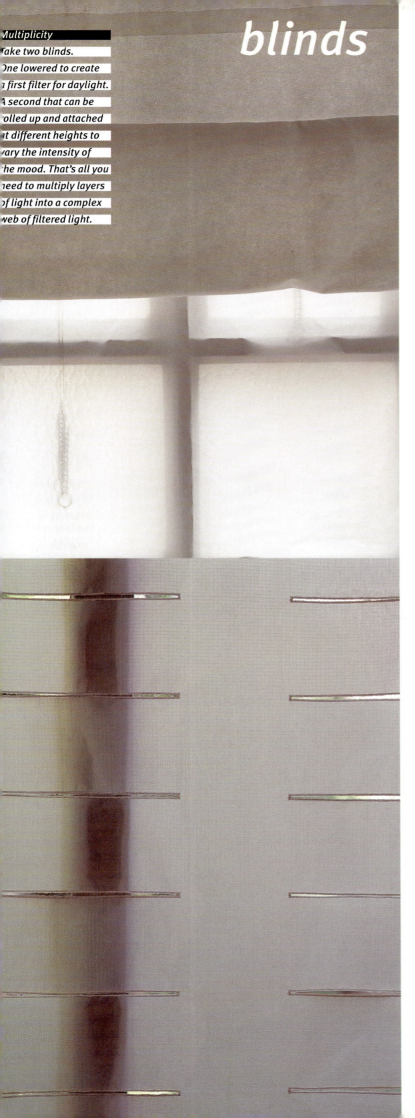

Multiplicity
Take two blinds. One lowered to create a first filter for daylight. A second that can be rolled up and attached at different heights to vary the intensity of the mood. That's all you need to multiply layers of light into a complex web of filtered light.

For centuries people regulated the light in their homes by opening or shutting the blinds in front of their windows. According to the season or the time of day the light and the warmth of the sun were manipulated by opening or shutting the blinds to obtain a perfect balance of light and comfort. Just remember your own experiences in the southern countries; the cool comfort on a hot summer day when the blinds were down and the energizing freshness and crispiness of a new day that welcomed you when the blinds were up again in the morning. The concept of using layers and blinds to control and filter the light can be a great inspiration to enliven your personal environment. Allowing you to reinvent, change and experience sensations and moods of well-being, playfulness and mystery all the year' round wherever you live.

Now you see me, now you don't...
Dressing up the window with stitched slits the world outside will reveal itself temptingly in brief and sudden glimpses.

Lightsuckers
The translucent sheets of plastic attached to the window with suction pads are an irresistible invitation to let your imagination run free. The tactile sensation of removing and attaching the suction pads in order to change the light-patterns creates the attraction of a sensuous game.

Air-bound
Shiny, translucent battons strung together form a sculptural curtain of colour and lightness. Invoking carefree summerholidays when gravity seems to loosen its grip and the sunlight presents itself in magical lemonade-colours.

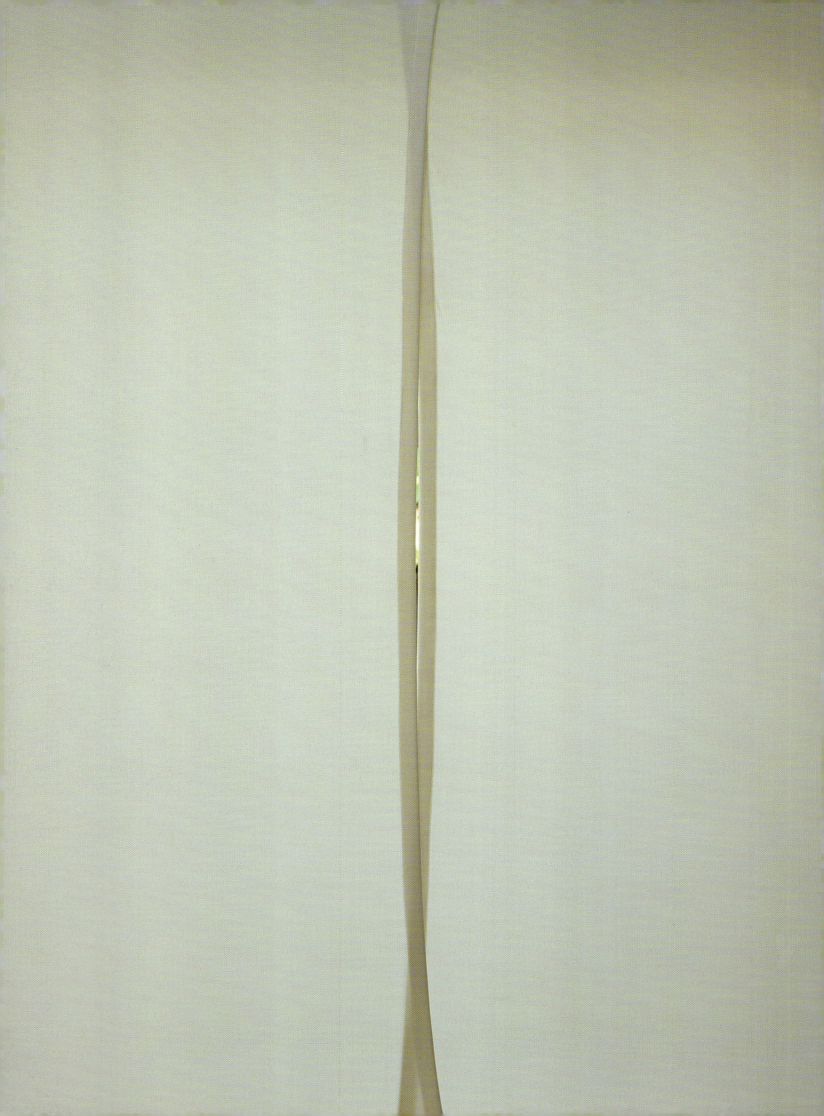

Translucent

Vague images appear, light and shades become more clear. The sun plays a game behind this translucent Lycra blind. A game of light, intensity, a game of elasticity. Tempted to see more clear, curiosity moves you to see behind the blind. The blind hesitates but then it jumps back underneath your hands.

Peeping Tom
A solid blind shuts out every beam of light. Only tiny rays of light are shining through peepholes giving Peeping Tom the exciting opportunity to watch secret pleasures and dark rituals.

INTERIOR VIEW 14

The young designer Chris Slutter (Enschede, 1972) shows a special interest in materials that stimulate the imagination. Like rubber that will always drop back to its original form: hence drubb. This self-invented word seemed to him the perfect term to describe his design for cupboards not even one inch deep and made of framed rubber. Drubb can be a glowing monochrome painting on your wall, a slim latex statue in your living-room or a very efficient and functional closet. Filled up with shoes, clothes, bottles or whatever you want to put away it becomes a three-dimensional, flexible object, a personal sculpture of your daily life changing with your moods and tastes. Unused these cupboards will always be more than just an empty closet or a redundant storage space. Filled, they are never the same but intrigue without imposing their presence. Like a mirror reflecting your lifestyle and not anyone else's the quality of the design consists in the endless opportunities it offers to change and personalise a simple, practical piece of furniture. At the same time it makes a convincing crossover between intelligent craftsmanship, clever interior design and modern art.

Text by **Marie Jeanne de Rooij, Chris Slutter Design** - Enschede/Holland (more information 00.31.53.433 80 09).

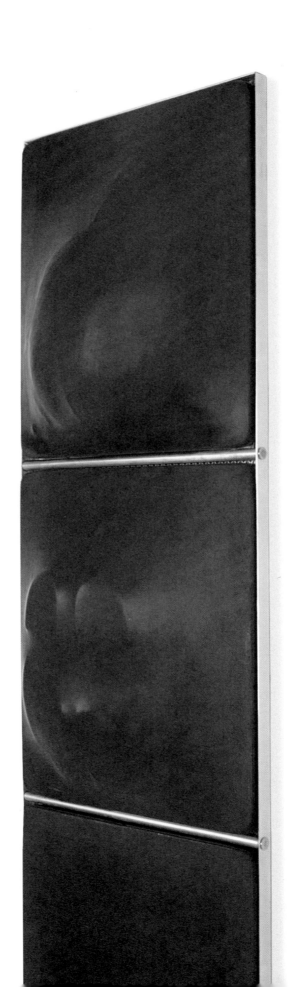

Drubb or Whatever you want me to be …

INTERIOR VIEW 14

As sophisticated computer technology becomes increasingly affordable, we are welcoming more and more hardware into our homes. Until now we have simply brought the computers and printers that we use in the office directly into our homes. Two recent projects emerging from workshops held by designers from IDEO Japan and manufacturers NEC and Epson have set out to question new technology and how we relate to it. ■ The workshops explored how a computer is incorporated into our everyday lives, its relationship with its environment, both when it is in use and when it is switched off. The designers were encouraged to express the present (as opposed to the future) and the human rather than the user. ■ The first project 'Whitebox', is an exploration of the personal computer, held by IDEO Japan with designers from computer giant NEC. The fundamental question to be examined was: "How can we connect a computer with our life?" ■ This was researched through three main themes: 'active memory', 'changing the mind' and 'found object, found material'. All of these proved beneficial in looking at design from a different perspective, although technological and market information provided by the computer company suggested that the 'rectangular box' dimensions will be with us for the next foreseeable future. ■ Recently the computer has become like a piece of clay, being moulded into different forms, often just to add some visual advantage over competitors but not having any effect on how we use the object or how we relate to it. Computer design seems to be calling to us, but it isn't saying much at all. ■ The designs were exhibited under the name 'Whitebox' in Tokyo, the exhibition featured video, music, models, text and photographs. All of the designs are based on the plastic box and displayed challenging solutions that hope to give more meaning to what has become an icon of the Twentieth Century. ■ The second project is 'Printables' which was conceived as a result of research done by manufacturer Epson into the changing market of colour printers. It was predicted that as digital technology became more sophisticated and readily available, no one would want to read books or magazines in their traditional printed format; instead we would be reading books on our palmtop computers and magazines and papers online. As with the idea of the 'paperless office' this is clearly not going to be the case. ■ We now have the ability to store vast amounts of information digitally, but we have not lost the love of holding a piece of paper, or of leafing through the pages of a book. Although we might browse through the Encyclopedia Britannica on CD, we still want to print pages, likewise when we research from the internet. The delivery of the information may have changed, but the end result is the same. ■ It was always predicted that colour printing would become a niche market, but research has shown that people are embracing the new breed of photo-quality colour printers at a rapid rate. The printers are being used by every member of the household, particularly for outputting from the internet and from digital cameras. Epson acknowledged that the current designs were closer to office machinery which was then migrating to the home. The object of the project was to reinvent the printer, this time in the context of domestic life and to look at our relation to the objects themselves, on a personal, social, intellectual and cultural level. ■ The series of design workshops that were held, with Naoto Fukasawa and Sam Hecht from IDEO in Japan with designers from Epson, dealt with the fundamental question of 'how to successfully position a colour printer into the home that embraces the subtle character and functional needs that a product should display'. Questions were asked about how to position and get the most from technology as it enters our homes as an outlet for displaying networked digital information and as a way of expressing creativity. ■ Their research showed that digital (PC) and analogue (print) are coexisting quite happily, rather than digital completely overtaking the latter. The blurred boundary between analogue and digital is the starting point for these designs which are aimed at exciting the human within the domestic environment and moving from designs intended for the office. ■ The aim was to create new possibilities through new solutions for a world that is constantly changing and with it our needs and aspirations. The designers were not concerned with minute changes to superficial features, since the project did not set out to be a styling exercise. They were concerned with what happens when a customer uses the product, not just what will make him or her buy it. ‡ During the workshops the designers focused on invention, striving for ideas that were both suitable and surprising, which would give rise to design that looks natural and 'undesigned'. Memory was another consideration and is often avoided when designing on a global scale, since companies are eager that products should not look too individual or have too local an appeal. The objects needed some sort of familiarity, but the designers were keen to avoid nostalgia. Memory is a way of injecting some meaning into the objects. ■ Until recently colour printing had to be sent out to a specialist, but the new range of printers give a quality that has never been available to the domestic market before, putting colour printing firmly in the hands of the individual. The designs are based around existing technology and featured the world's first six colour ink jet printer, which allows more colours to be printed and provides a closer colour match between screen and print.

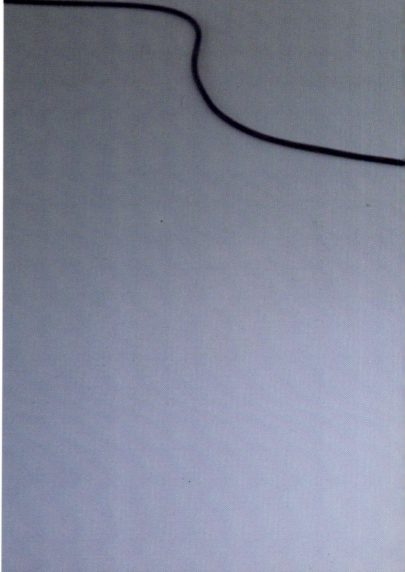

whitebox project

INTERIOR VIEW 14

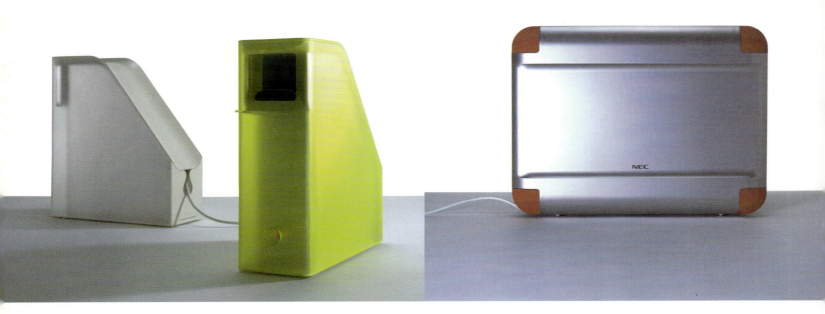

Sam Hecht has produced a computer that is based on the file - representing anonymity and endless possibilities. The computer stands up, using less precious desk space and the disk drive is parallel to the user, allowing the label on the disk to be seen whilst it is in the computer. The power button is in a deep recess that glows softly when the power is on and the cabling is hidden deep into the moulding at the back. It does not scream for attention or look at odds with its environment; it is efficient and compact. ■ In contrast to this, Naoto Fukasawa has designed a computer that is placed on the floor and looks like a plant, rooted in a container. Instead of being hidden, the cables are wrapped around a pole like ivy and the lid reveals the cable connections. The disk is inserted like a plant label and the power indicator is at the top of the pole, a bit like a flower. The design emphasises the importance of the screen, the processor can be put out of the way on the floor. ■ Hiroe Hiyame has looked at the way we often buy a computer for its appearance instead of its technology and he has designed a computer that is made up of separate components which are then assembled in a 'shopping bag'. We can choose our favourite brands and change and recycle the different pieces when we want to upgrade them. ■ Computers are often very fragile and difficult to move. Kenichi Tsuchiyah has created a robust computer that can be easily moved around and removes the need for extra protection - the computer has become its own packaging.

Masahiko Kobayashi's design features the printer mechanism sandwiched between two cardboard sheets. Like a book, the printer can be placed vertically when not in use, horizontally when it is in use. It is designed to recall the opening of a book and challenge our perception of the printer as a static object - this one is designed to be handled, moved and stored. ■ Naoto Fukaswa has connected the printer with it's own wastebasket, implying that there will always be prints that are not right and that we will dispose of several sheets before we get the perfect print. The paper is delivered vertically and lays on a thin wire support. ■ Sam Hecht has focused on the developing process. Just like a photographic print, the print is ejected from the bottom of the machine into a tray where it is enriched to photo quality. The photo-kit analogy is carried further, with a wire mechanism that acts like a frame and allows the printed results to be displayed and admired. ■ Hirokazu Yamano has developed a printer that is draped in cloth with each printout, like a note slipped secretly under a door. The ink head vibrates gently the fabric casing when coming out magically from underneath the white handkerchief. ■ Yoshihiro Tatara has designed a long horizontal slab that is raised above the desk and has the option of a 4 leg support - the printer then becomes a surface that can be used to house peripherals. The paper is kept at the back, pushed out at the front and displayed on top, which keeps the paper flat. ■ The 7 designs have been developed into fully functioning products and will be shown at London's Design Museum and at the OZONE gallery in Tokyo, and a book titled 'Printables', has also been produced in a limited edition of 200. All of these designs offer thought-provoking solutions to the question of how technology can relate more directly to he people who use it.

Bless this, bless that

Step by step, Desiree Heiss and Ines Kaag keep developing their unconventional design approach since the day they launched their first fashion concepts now 4 years ago. That first **BLESS** cooperation quickly led to a seasonless collection of limited series of 'things' with each of them one common characteristic: seducing the consumer interacting creatively within the product. **BLESS** N°02 was a limited edition of sixty sets of disposable T-shirts and is completely sold out. **BLESS** N°06 consists of customisable footwear with 250 different variations. In the meantime, they sell stylefree bag systems, wearable make-up and even style-corrupting subscriptions. The following is a glimpse of **BLESS** N°07, a complete range of 'living-room conquerors'. As they put it themselves: "A living-room needs to live and develop its destiny. A gradual transformation of personal values keeps existing and adapts to fresh areas that mark a moment of consciousness. The charm of old furniture —as experienced companions— react with environmental accessories on the way to a personal living concept. Their desire to grow with you can be satisfied through a handsome balance. **BLESS** our home." For all of those charmed by the innocent and harmless image of **BLESS**, a word of advice: the mixture of its limited distribution, the hypnotising descriptions and the surreal product approach might be a much more premeditated strategy than one would first believe. Before you know it, you might be eating **BLESS** food, driving Bless automobiles and watching **BLESS** TV. Beware.

CHAIRWEAR B An extremely flexible jersey-hill, that expands while you're sitting down, limited to 250
1 pull the 2 front legs of the chair through the trimmed framed holes of the black jersey cover
2 put the sticks in line with the chairlegs to end properly in the inside fixed pvc corners **3** fasten the zipper
4 use the one-way clasps to fix the sticks on the chairlegs **5** sit down

CHAIRWEAR C A vivid transparent box for a chair that twists and alters its shape while it is being used and with a memory effect that allows it to regain its original shape once released (get-up support). limited to 50.
1 unfold the black box **2** find an object to cover; anything which is used for sitting down will do; don't hesitate to squeeze it while you're sitting, it gets up together with you anyway. photography **Kenshu Shintsubo** model **Kate Frei** text **Wouter Wiels**

photos by **Ingmar Swalue** @ Solar, assisted by **Mandy Pieper**, text by **Marie Jeanne de Rooij**, styling by **Sabine C. Jansen** @ House of Orange, assisted by **Trine Komum**, interior styling by **Kasia Gatkowska & Bas Andrea** @ House of Orange, hair and make up by **Ingrid Boekel** @ House of Orange assisted by **Renata Mandic**, models **Asha, Olga and Bart-Jan** @ de Boekers, **Maartje** @ Ulla Models, **Joris** @ Paparazi, **Bas, Thirza, Sam, Bruin and Zep**, funeral dinner by **Marije Vogelzang**, clothes by **Analik, Aziz, Saskia van Drimmelen, So, Tessa Koops and Storm**, location **Loods 6**, Thanks to **Pet & Jeanet**

the white feast for the dead

r Marije Vogelezang it started as a school project (Design Academy Eindhoven) with the theme 'white'. White is the colour of death in many cultures. After a life colourful, decisive and sometimes painful changes we reach the final threshold to eternal nothingness. White is the perfect non-colour to express symbolically e last stage of our existence. Going back to where we started we reach a blank, the unknown where time, space and matter no longer rule. ■ People have always ed to mark this transition with rituals in which family, friends and other members of the community participate. Although many cultures have developed aborate rituals, in Western Europe - especially in the calvinist North - the tendency towards down-to-earth, sober ceremonies has become the general proach to say our last goodbyes to our loved ones. ■ Impressed and inspired by the funerary customs of non-Western cultures Marije Vogelezang wanted to evelop an alternative for the loveless coffee-cake routine of her own culture. Three times already she has organised a white funeral-lunch, a performance for nich she designs everything up to the very last detail; the crockery, the clothes, the tablelinen, the furniture. Everything has to be white, even the food must esent itself in tones and shades of white. ■ Vogelezang has been experimenting extensively with ingredients, recipes, flavours and combinations to reach the stive and serene celebration she is looking for. The mourners are invited to share a light meal of several exquisite, carefully prepared dishes made of chicken, h, mushrooms and rice. The table is set in advance so nothing will disturb the ritual not even the sound of cuttlery, since everybody is supposed to eat with his her hands. In this atmophere of lightness and serenity she is convinced people can truly concentrate on memories of the deceased, cherish the special oments and comfort each other. A white feast to celebrate a sad occasion and to honour the dead with all the purity and beauty we, the living, possess. ■

▼

"Botanic" means deep lush colours, but that's just part of the story. "Cuddling Memories" has to do with soft warm textures, but it's also a palette and range of materials. "Rural Roots" is the name given to the farming trend, the one with sober contrasts. "Functional Essentials" takes on the nomadic impulse in all our lives, while the "Industrial Essentials" have to do with simple, everyday luxury. And "Silent Tactilities" refers to the paring down of visual overload, something which we all welcome with relief.

What to know more? Every one of these six lifestyle trends is illustrated and explained in the Interior View Lifestyle Colour Cards for 2000-2001. Divided into four panels, each card communicates one trend. First the "Colour Range," supplies the basis for the trend. Then, the "Influence" panel, illustrates the trend in images, providing both inspiration and the emotional tone. Next, the "Product" panel lays out the materials, and finally, the "Accents" are communicated in an icon image and palette. The cards fit into a smart, durable binder, each with its own accompanying text. Clear, accessible, provocative, the Interior View Lifestyle Colour Cards provide a nifty shorthand for the colour, style and materials that you want to be aware of. The suggestive lay-out and description give you the flexibility you need to adapt the Lifestyle Cards to any interior project. They'll supply you with ideas, confirm your intuition, and revitalize your own, personal view.

milan 2000. what's up? As in a moment of calm before a huricane or an eruption ; design gently floats in. An evolution waiting for the big bang of a new era to explode into our interiors. Some small new things here and there announced the arrival of the rebellions, the colourful, the outsider. But most design was soft and safe and subtle and perfect and balanced and utterly boring. Too well made, too well finished, too well designed most brands sent a message of distinguished deja-vu. Some slow motion is to be noted: from warmish cream to cold light neutrals, from dark wood to blond or medium grey, from off-whites to intense and bluish whites, from stainless to matt metals, from orange to shocking pink plastics, and also from texture to more texture including loop fabrics, from carpets to more carpets to even wall-to-wall carpeting, from felt to more felt and even moulded felts from plastic to more plastics in variations in tactility, from classic bedding to the trendy 24 hour bed from bath to a total lifestyle (including accessories and a devine selection of tiles at Bofti). Some trends reached critical mass and helped us to create the following pages;

dutch the coming of age of the Dutch design mentality, the arrival of Evident Design, with Droog Design, Dutch Individuals and some outsiders like Edward van Vliet, Harry and Camila and Marre Moerel

white this issue of Interior View is right on to this moment of bliss in which colour is absent, details are hidden, material tactile and design spheric; the importance of noiseless, voiceless, absorbing Blind Design

fluo The name of Hella Jongerius becomes a household name, her skill to fuse the past with the future and ethno with techno will make her one of the leading figures of the early 21st century.

naive stepping aside, playing games, having fun, jumping and moving, versatile and fantastic some design plays on the nostalgic cord of our childhood memories; Making us wish to be forever young. Still a kid, master Gaetano Pesce surprised us with new projects like lighting and childrens furniture. Allowing small budgets to be part of the dream.

compact recycled and recomposed papers, felts, plastics, woods and concretes look new in matters of alternative and avantgardist design. The way to use these materials is in moulded and welded organic shapes giving an edge to soft design.

armchair The recent wave of designer hotels has brought along a long forgotten friend, the small and cosy armchair adorn a suite or a grand entrance. They come in all materials and all colours but they are all smaller, prettier and sexier then ever before. The new armchair is upright and perly, almost like a person inviting flirtatious behaviour.

dutch

white

fluo

naive

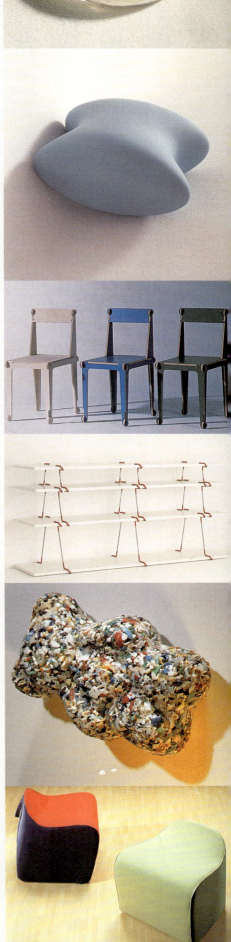

compact

armchair

LIST OF AGENTS AND LOCAL OFFICES

DISTRIBUTION MANAGEMENT
mode... information • Heinz Kramer GmbH • Pilgerstr. 20 • D-51491 Overath
Tel. 02206-6007-0 • Fax 02206-6007-17 • e-mail: mode.info@t-online.de • http://www.modeinfo.com

AUSTRALIA
Europress Distributors Pty. Ltd.
Unit 3, 123 McEvoy Street
Alexandria NSW 2015
Tel.: 02 - 9698 49 22
Fax : 02 - 9698 76 75
e-mail: europress@acay.com.au

BELGIE
mode...information Belgium
Hubert Frère-Orbanlaan 644/649
9000 Gent
Tel.: 09-224 43 87
Fax : 09-224 43 95

BRAZIL
Lexus
Books & CIA
Rua Henrique Ongari, 156/B
05037-150 São Paulo SP
Tel: 011-861 18 72
Fax: 011-861 00 95

HB Revistas Tecnicas Intern. Ltda.
Caixa Postal 61034
BR 05001-970 São Paulo SP
Tel: 011-826 67 77
Fax: 011-36 66 64 35
e-mail: hb.revistas@nvc.com.br

CANADA
Catherine Berry & Associates
Fashion Forecasting Resources
68 Dean Avenue
Guelph, Ontario N1G1LA
Tel: 519 - 822 43 39
Fax: 519 - 822 43 96

Fashion Resources
4842 Roslyn Avenue
Montréal, Québec H3W2L2
Tel: 512 - 731 10 11
Fax: 514 - 731 50 11

Speedimpex Canada Inc.
155 Deerhide Crescent
Weston, Ontario M9M2Z2
Tel: 416 - 741 75 55
Tlx: 6527401 speedimpex tor
Fax: 416 - 741 46 34

CHINA
China Textile Information
Institute
10/F China Textile Mansion
(Oriental Garden Hotel)
N°6 South St., Dongzhimen
TJ-1000 27 Beijing
Tel.: 010 - 641 682 45
Fax: 010 - 641 597 02
e-mail: textiles@ctii.com.cn

CZECH REPUBLIC
Linea Ubok
Na Prikope 27
113 49 Praha 1
Tel: 02 - 242 28 788
Fax: 02 - 242 28 293

DANMARK
PEJ Gruppen
Hybenvej 4, Hammerum
7400 Herning
Tel.: 097-11 89 00
Fax : 097-11 85 11
e-mail: info@pejgruppen.dk

Forhandler Service & Dansk
Bladdistribution A/S
Ved Amagerbanen 9
2300 Kobenhavn S
Tel.: 031 - 54 34 44
Fax: 031 - 54 60 64
e-mail: db@danskblad.dk

DEUTSCHLAND
mode...information
Heinz Kramer GmbH
Pilgerstr. 20
51491 Overath
Tel.: 02206-6007-0
Fax : 02206-6007-17
e-mail: mode.info@t-online.de

Showroom München
Gaby Kilian
Bäckerstr. 34f
81241 München
Tel.: 089-8 88 88 05
Fax : 089-8 34 39 56

ESPAÑA
José Isart Solanellas
Plaza Tetuan 6, 1.°
08010 Barcelona
Tel.: 03-2 65 60 11
Fax : 03-2 65 51 18

FRANCE
mode...information S.A.
67, boulevard de Sébastopol
75002 Paris
Tél.: 01 - 40 13 81 50
Fax : 01 - 40 13 81 68
e-mail: mode.information.france
@goffornet.com

Ginette Haack
6 Cité Paradis
75010 Paris
Tel.: 1-40 22 02 69
Fax : 1-45 23 07 65

United Publishers
Corinne Lassalle
30 Bld Saint Jaques
75014 Paris
France
Tel: 1-44 08 68 88
fax: 1-43317791

GREAT BRITAIN
Dawson Subscription service
Cannon House
Folkestone
Kent CT 19 5EE
Tel.: 01303 - 85 01 01
Tlx.: 96392
Fax: 01303 - 85 04 40

K.M. Associates
Margaret Kinsey & Carole May
174, Andrewes House
Barbican
London EC2Y 8BA
Tel.: 0171 - 638 82 67
Fax: 0171 - 638 97 76

mode...information Ltd.
First Floor Eastgate House
16-19 Eastcastle Street
London W1N 7PA
Tel.: 0171-436 01 33
Fax : 0171-436 02 77
e-mail: modeinformation@
  dial.webs.co.uk

R.D.Franks Ltd.
Market Place, Oxford Circus
London W1N 8EJ
Tel.: 0171-636 12 44/5/6
Tlx.: 8955855 kenlin g
Fax : 0171-436 49 04

HELLAS
Inter Fashion Express
Thanos Komninos & Co.
1-5, Lekka Street
10563 Athens
Tel.: 01 - 322 63 78
  01 - 323 78 76
Fax : 01 - 323 78 76
e-mail: komninos@acropolis.net
8, Lagadastr.
54630 Thessaloniki
Tel.: 031- 52 95 05

HONG KONG
Fashion Consultant Ltd.
20/FL, Flat B, Causeway Tower
16-22 Causeway Road
HK Hong-Kong
Tel.: 25 76 17 37
Fax: 28 95 00 62

INDIA
Bombay Subscription Agency
Mahavir Apt. nr. Bhatia Hosp.
Tardeo Rd
Bombay 400 007
Tel: 022 - 37 77 29
Fax: 022 - 30 72 229
e-mail:
baraash@bom4.van1.net.in

Get & Gain Centre
301, Sagar Shopping Centre, 3rd fl.
76, J.P. Road,
Andheri (W)
Bombay 400 058
Tel: 022 - 620 34 31/ 624 59 98
Fax: 022 - 624 27 06

Honesty
Subscription Agency
Kalbadvi Road
45 / 47 Dr M.B. Welkar Street
Bombay 400 002
Tel: 022 - 201 76 04
  022 - 201 86 32
Fax: 022 - 208 69 59

Super Journals PVT. Ltd.
169, Sant Nagar, East of Kailash
New-Dehli- 110 065
Tel.: 011 - 623 11 18
  011 - 623 63 13
  011 - 623 95 21
Fax: 011 - 648 56 48
e-mail: superj@del2.vsnl.net.in

ISLAND
IB Press Distribution Ltd
Sudurlandsbraut 32
IS - 108 Reijkjavic
Tel: 05 - 33 22 11
Fax: 05 - 33 22 12

ISRAEL
Librairie Francaise Alcheh
30 Burla Street -P.O.Box 23758
Tel Aviv
Tel.+ Fax: 03-69 94 526

ITALIA
mode...information Italia S.r.l.
Via Clemente Prudenzio 16
20138 Milano
Tel.: 002-58 01 22 82
Fax : 002-58 01 22 87
e-mail: mode.info@planet.it

MALAYSIA
Leng Peng Fashion Book Centre
see Singapore

MEXICO
mode... information Mexico
Mara Zillgens S.A. de C.V.
Dr Carmona y Valle 5 Ap. 401
Col. Doctores Cuauhtemoc
06720 Mexico DF
Tel.: 05 - 578 74 63
Fax: 05 - 578 74 63

NEDERLAND
Appletizer Forecast,
colcur&Information centre-
Patrick Appels
De Els 6
5141 HH Waalwijk
Tel.: 0416-34 32 73
Fax : 0416-34 00 77
e-mail: appletiz@xs4all.nl

NEW ZEALAND
The Fashion Bookery
Norma Hollis
P.O. Box 35, 621 Browns Bay
Auckland 10
Tel.: 09 - 415 56 60
Fax : 09 - 415 56 50
e-mail:
the.fashion.bookery@clear.net.nz

NIPPON
Attrait Fashion Inc.
Osaka Higashi P.O. Box 650
Zeniya Dai-ichi Bldg. 4 F
1-6-19 Azuchi-machi Chuo-ku
Osaka 541 - 0052
Tel: 06 - 6264 13 09
Tlx: 65204 attrait j
Fax 06 - 6264 13 16

Bookmans & Co Ltd
1 - 18 Toyosaki, 3-Chome
Kita-Ku
Osaka 531
Te;: 06 - 63 71 41 64
Fax: 06 - 63 71 41 74

Itochu Fashion System Co Ltd.
contact: Ms. Itoi
2-5-1 Kita-aoyama, Minato-Ku
Tokyo 107
Tel: (81) 3 - 3497 86 50
Fax: (81) 3 - 3497 80 31

Kaigai Inc.
No. 5-30, Hiroshiba-cho Suita-shi
Osaka 564
Tel: 06 - 63 85 52 31
Tlx: 64198 kaigai j
Fax: 06 -63 85 52 34

Taiyo Trading Co. Ltd.
Miki Bldg., 3F, 2-12-12 Shibuya,
Shibuya-Ku
Tokyo 150
Tel: 03-34 06 72 21
Tlx: 2424120 taiyo j
Fax: 03-3 54 85 93 33

Talk International Co. Ltd.
4-11 Minami-hommachi 2-chome,
Chuo-Ku
Osaka 541 - 0054
Tel.: 06 - 62 62 32 13
Fax: 06 - 62 62 32 76

Toyo Inc.
Semba P.O. Box 183, Chuo Ku
Osaka 541
Tel: 06-245 08 46
Tlx: 63839 helpmate j
Fax: 06-245 07 09

Yohan Western Publications
Distribution Agency
14-9 Okubo 3-chome,
Shinjuku-ku
Tokyo 169
Tel.: 03-32 08 01 81-7
Tlx.: 234818 yohan j
Fax : 03-32 08 53 08

NORGE
Narvesen Distribusjon
Postbox 6219, Etterstad
0602 Oslo
Tel: 02-2 57 30 10
Tlx: 76835 nordi n
Fax : 02-2 68 69 24

PORTUGAL
mode... information
Masolo Representacoes, Lda
P.O.B. 38 - Louro
4761 V.N. Famalicao
Tel.: 052 - 30 07 00
Fax: 052 - 30 07 09
e-mail: sepol@mail.telepac.pt

SCHWEIZ
Trend Information
Anita Billing
Bruggerstraße 37b
Merker-Fabrik-Areal
5400 Baden
Tel: 056 222 66 22
Fax: 056 221 78 11

SINGAPORE
Basheer graphic books
Block 231 #04-19 Bras Basah
Complex
Bain Street
Singapore 180231
Tel: 336 08 10
Fax: 334 19 50

Leng Peng Fashion Book Centre
BLK. 3007, Ubi Road 1 06-426
Singapore 408 701
Tel.: 7 46 20 57
Fax: 7 42 46 86

SUID AFRICA
International Trand Information
Block A Loudon Park
8, St Marys Road
3610 Kloof / Durban
Tel.: 031 - 764 66 16
Fax: 031 - 764 30 90
e-mail: iti@ico.owl.co.za

SUOMI
Akateeminen Kirjakauppa
Tom Backman/PK 6
P.O. BOX 147
00381 Helsinki
Tel: 09 - 121 42 41
Fax: 09 - 121 43 30
e-mail: tom.backman
  @stockmann.fi

Mode Gallery B.A.J. Oy
Kicka Jokisalo
Jaakontie 20 as 1
28500 Pori
Tel.: 02 - 633 42 87
Fax : 02 - 633 42 33

Suomalainen
Kirjakauppa Oy
P.O. Box 2
01641 Vantaa 64
Tel: 0 - 852 751
Tlx: 121841 suomk sf
Fax: 0 - 852 79 90

SVERIGE
mode...information Scandinavia
P.O. Box 12104
402 41 Göteborg
Office: Klippan 1 C
414 51 Göteborg
Tel.: 031 - 12 44 56
Fax: 031 - 12 35 45
e-mail:
mode.info@colourhouse.se

Press Stop
Press Stop Gruppen Bror
Lundberg AB
PO Box 19063
104 32 Stockholm
Tel: 08 - 612 91 80
Fax: 08 - 612 27 90
e-mail:
jonny.lonn@brorlundberg.se

TAIWAN
Fashion Magazine Co., Ltd
P.O. Box 47-146
Taipei
Tel: 02 - 25 96 99 64
Fax: 02 - 25 92 20 50
E-mail: davidwu1@ms8.hinet.net

Navigator Magazine Press Co.
8th floor, No.300 Ming-Shen
West Road
ROC- Taipei/Taiwan
Tel.: 02 - 556 91 89
Fax: 02 - 556 91 69

New Time Fashion Magazine
P.O Box 9 - 210
Taipei
Tel.: 02- 556 92 66
Fax: 02- 558 99 37

TÜRKIYE
Kültür Pazarlama
P.O.B. 1191
80007 Karaköy / Istanbul
Tel: 212 - 248 45 59
  212 - 247 58 55
Fax: 212 - 234 23 10

URUGUAY
Graffiti S.r.l.
La Libreria de la Imagen
Convencion 1366, Local 8
11500 Montevideo
Tel.: 02 - 92 29 76

USA
Dorothy Waxman
Waxman Associates
90 Riverside Drive
New York, NY 10024
Tel: 212 - 724 3825
Fax: 212 - 724 3129

Ebsco
American library College
1762 Westwood Blvd.
Los Angeles
CA 90024-5622
Tel: 205 - 991 66 00
Fax: 205 - 991 14 79

International Fashion
Publications
California Mart
110E 9th St., B 286
Los Angeles, CA 90079
Tel: 213 - 622 56 63
Fax: 213 - 623 18 09
Toll free Nr: 800 347 2589

Margit Publications
1412 Broadway - Room #1102
New York NY 10018
Tel.: 212-3 02 51 37
Fax: 212-9 44 87 57
e-mail: margit@mpnews.com

Overseas Publishers
Representatives
1328 Broadway, Suite 645
New York, N.Y. 10001-2121
Tel.: 212 - 564 39 54
Fax : 212 - 465 89 38
Toll Free Number Hotline:
1-800 666 Mags (6247)
e-mail: opr1328@soho.los.com

Speedimpex USA Inc.
35-02 48th Avenue
USA-Long Island City,
N.Y. 11101
Tel.: 718-3 92 74 77
Tlx.: 667265 speed via wui
Fax : 718-3 61 08 15